Ballet Russe

PAGEANT OF HISTORY

PAGEANT OF HISTORY   EDITOR: JOHN GROSS

Arnold L. Haskell

Ballet Russe

The Age of Diaghilev

WEIDENFELD AND NICOLSON 5 WINSLEY STREET LONDON W1

© 1968 by Arnold L. Haskell

SBN 297 76263 x
Designed by Hewat/Swift/Walters Ltd
for George Weidenfeld and Nicolson Limited, London

Printed in Great Britain by Ebenezer Baylis & Son Limited
The Trinity Press, Worcester, and London

FOR JAN AND BORIS WITH LOVE

Contents

	Foreword	9
1	Du Côté de Guermantes – Paris 1906	11
2	Roots – Russia 1872–90	16
3	A Provincial in the Capital – Russia 1890–95	27
4	The World of Art – Russia 1899–1904	33
5	First Contacts with the Ballet – Russia 1899	37
6	The Russian Exhibition – Paris 1906	53
7	Diaghilev and Fokine – Russia and Paris 1909–13	56
8	Successes and scandals	77
9	The Last Years	100
10	In Retrospect	115
	Notes on further reading	121
	Index	123

Acknowledgements

The author and publishers would like to thank the people and institutions below for permission to reproduce the photographs mentioned before their names.

39, 66 (*above*), Ashmolean Museum; 17, 20 (*below right and bottom right*), 21, 22 (*top right and bottom right*), 46, 68 (*above*), British Museum; 83, 118, Richard Buckle; 109 (*above*), Central Press Photos; 13, 31, 54, 63, 70, 73, 78, 81, 91, Librairie Stock; 44/5, Musée des Arts Decoratifs (*photo Hélène Adant*); 24, Museum of Modern Art, New York (*Gift of Edward M. M. Warburg*); 19, 93, 110, 112, Radio Times Hulton Picture Library; 20 (*above and below*), 22 (*left*), 23, 42, 43 (*above and below*), 44 (*left*), 48 (*above and below*), 65 (*above and below*), 66 (*below*), 67 (*above and below*), 68 (*below*), 86, 87 (*above and below*), 88 (*left and right*), 95 (*above*), 101, 102, Victoria and Albert Museum; 41 (*above and left*), 85 (*above and below*), 94, 95 (*below*), 96 (*above and below*, 109 (*below*), 111 (*above and below*), Wadsworth Atheneum.

Foreword

I was fortunate enough to know Diaghilev and most of the leading figures in this monograph, in particular Walter Nouvel and Michael Larionov. When writing Diaghilev's biography in 1934 I discussed his work at length in over two hundred interviews. The problem here has been one of selection and evaluation. In treating the subject again after an interval of thirty years, I have been amazed by the size of the figure that emerges and by his undoubted creative quality. Thirty years ago this was still hotly debated. His collaborators, jealous for their own reputations, stressed his drive, his will-power and his flair. Now Diaghilev has vanished and no one has stepped into his shoes. It is through this void that we can realise that Diaghilev was the spokesman for the aesthetic of a period, one that was vastly exciting and on which the aesthetic of the present is firmly based. We can also see that this was no haphazard affair but that the Diaghilev we knew in Western Europe from 1909 to 1929 was already fully formed when he gave his first ballet season. There were times when he was prevented from following a consistent path and retreated into triviality, but today we can appreciate with what skill, wit and taste even the trivia were put together.

1
Du Côté de Guermantes Paris 1906

The Diaghilev era lasted for twenty years, spanning a world war and the greatest social upheaval of modern times. It changed the vision of a generation through its influence on painting, music, ballet and stagecraft. Yet Diaghilev himself practised none of these arts. He was, in fact, a failed musician, a revolutionary who was firmly rooted in tradition, a dilettante who was professional to his fingertips in a profession that was born and that died with him. His whole career was a paradox. He was seemingly reckless yet painstaking to a degree, a businessman who cared nothing for money or personal possessions. From the age of twenty the list of his collaborators reads like an index to the cultural history of the first three decades of the century.

Let us meet him in Paris one day in the spring of 1906 at a reception given by the Comtesse de Greffulhe (Marcel Proust's Madame de Guermantes), in her famous salon in the rue d'Astorg. She was the greatest patron of the arts in the Paris of that period, and very little took place without her active intervention. Among her guests that day were Gabriel Astruc, a close friend of Marcel Proust's, and a comparatively unknown Russian, Serge Diaghilev. He was a striking looking man, with his large head, his sensual lips and carefully trimmed circumflex moustache, his monocle and the white mesh growing out of the thick brown bristly hair that had earned him the nickname of *Chinchilla*.

'I have brought you two together,' said Madame de Greffulhe, 'because M. de Diaghilev is organising an exhibition of Russian art at the Salon d'Automne and wishes at the same time to arrange some concerts of Russian music.' Diaghilev greeted Astruc in his most honeyed tones. 'Je vous connais, Monsieur' – and he recited a list of Astruc's triumphs, among them the Paris débuts of Arthur Rubinstein, Wanda Landowska and Mata Hari.

The two men became firm friends. They had much in common: ambition and drive, mellowed by considerable charm, a love of the sensational and a strong sense of the importance of social relations. The word *impresario* was totally inadequate to describe the functions of either man.

The first result of this meeting was five concerts of Russian music at the Opéra in 1907 under the patronage of M. Nelidov, the Russian Ambassador, and a young minister, Aristide Briand. The music of Moussorgsky caused a sensation.

The following year saw, under the same auspices, the Paris début of Feodor Chaliapin in a fabulous production of *Boris Godounov* with décors by Golovin, Yuon and Benois. Chaliapin's personal success was such that it revolutionised the whole conception of operatic acting and production. As a result of this season Diaghilev made many valuable connections and two close friendships that were to prove deep, lasting and constructive: with the Princesse de Polignac and Misia Edwardes, later Misia Sert.

Misia, the confidante of every painter and musician of her day, was from then on to be Diaghilev's greatest friend. (She was with him in Venice when he died.) 'Unfortunately I have no sister,' he wrote to her, 'so that all my affection is centred on you.' She had been so moved by the first performance of *Boris* that she had been unable to sit still in her seat and had gone to stand on the gallery stairs till the curtain fell.

'The production, the scenery and the costumes were more sumptuous than anything the Opéra had known, and Diaghilev himself had supervised the acting and the lighting . . . I left the theatre with the feeling that something in my life had been changed . . . The music haunted me and each time it was given I was there . . . as enthusiastic as ever. I made all the propaganda I could and brought with me all those I loved . . .'

Self-portrait of Jean Cocteau

She did more, buying up all the empty seats so that Diaghilev might 'have the encouraging illusion of a financial success'. When they met she said that she soon felt that of all her friends he was the closest and that his affection was indispensable. He consulted her at every step. She introduced him to all the young musicians she had met through Jean Cocteau, who was also to make the complete journey with Diaghilev. 'Jean, astonish me,' he said to Cocteau, and Cocteau never failed him. The influential Diaghilev circle was taking shape.

When the opera season had ended the friends dined together at Paillard to celebrate its triumphs. During dessert Astruc told Diaghilev how impressed he had been by the décors and ensembles of the Polish scene and most especially by the polonaise.

'You seem to me to love the dance,' said Diaghilev. 'What a pity that you have never seen an evening of ballet in St Petersburg. In France you do not take the ballet as seriously as we do. It is incomplete as an art. You have many ballerinas but you know nothing of great male dancers.' He then went on to rhapsodise over Nijinsky, 'a veritable lion of the dance who can cover the stage in two bounds,' and his great partner Anna Pavlova, '*ou plutôt, La Pavlova*', over the great maestro Cecchetti and the choreographer of genius, Fokine. 'And don't forget that it was the King of France who in allowing the greatest of his choreographers to visit Russia founded the Russian school.'

Astruc, inspired by Diaghilev's enthusiasm, immediately said, 'I shall bring Pavlova, Nijinsky and Fokine to Paris next season.' It was Diaghilev who doubted whether the French public could stand a whole evening of ballet. Astruc, however, was already convinced. The next day the contract was signed and Astruc set

A sketch of Diaghilev by Larionov

out on his *tournée de Mécènes*, securing guarantees of a hundred thousand francs from Isaac de Camondo, André Benac, Henry Deutsh de la Meurthe, Henri de Rothschild, Basil Zaharoff and André Raffalovitch. Diaghilev had proved himself. He was to bring to Paris a ballet of his conception, one that Russia had never seen.

Who was this man who at the age of thirty-six deliberately set out to conquer the most sophisticated city in the world? Or rather, since he was always a realist, to conquer 'the thirty people who alone could provide an artist with his passport'?

2
Roots
Russia
1872/90

Sergei Pavlovich Diaghilev was born in 1872 in the province of Novgorod. His father, a member of the county aristocracy, was a colonel in the *chevalier gardes* and his mother, who died in giving him birth, also came from a distinguished family. The fact of his noble ancestry was certainly an important influence in his life, endowing him with self-assurance from the earliest days. His father, often away from home, had little direct influence on him, though like all the Diaghilevs he had great charm and a love and understanding of music. When he was ten the family settled in Perm; this again is important, for it meant that when the young provincial came to the capital it was an adventure and a challenge. The greatest influence of all, however, was that of his stepmother, Elena Valerianovna Panaieva, whom he called 'the best woman in the world'. She came from an exceedingly musical family. Her sister Panaieva Kartseva was a pupil of Pauline Viardot, and her father had built a private theatre where Italian opera was performed by the finest singers of the day. She brought up Sergei Pavlovich from birth, divined and fostered his great gifts, taught him self-discipline and developed his extraordinary will-power. ' "I cannot" is a phrase you must forget. When one wants to one always can.' The Diaghilev family was the most important in Perm and, even as a schoolboy, Sergei Pavlovich realised this. 'He was truly a *barin*,' said a school friend, 'and the masters treated him with deference.' They were gratified to be invited to dine at 'the big house' which was the centre of the town's social and artistic activities. The guests often sat down fifty at table on the long wooden verandah.

A portrait by Léon Bakst of Diaghilev and his old nanny, who presided over the samovar.

Costume designs by Benois for a courtier and the Marquis in *Le Pavillon d'Armide*.

opposite Décor by Alexandre Benois for *Le Pavillon d'Armide*, performed in St Petersburg in 1907 and in Paris in 1909. It was the first collaboration by the group.

Anna Pavlova. Diaghilev never forgave her for leaving his company to make her own career.

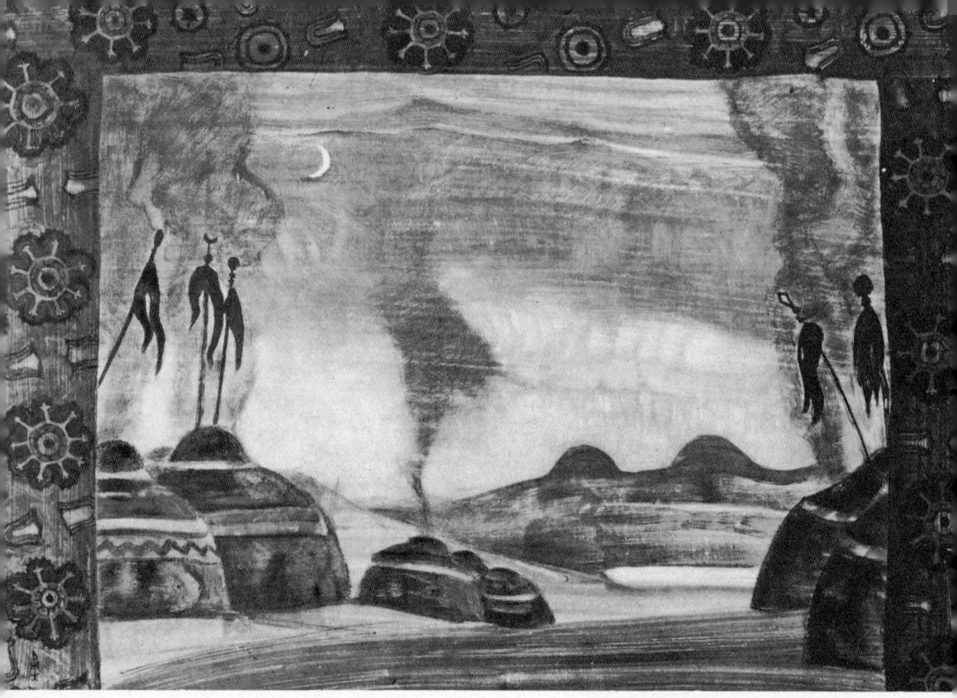

The Polovtsian camp, from *Prince Igor*, 1909. The settings were by N. Roerich.

МІРЪ ИСКУССТВА

The first page of the first volume of *Mir Iskusstva* (The World of Art), edited by Diaghilev, St Petersburg, 1899. This magazine fulfilled its mission of forming a bridge between the arts in Russia and the rest of Europe, and in a sense the ballet continued that work.

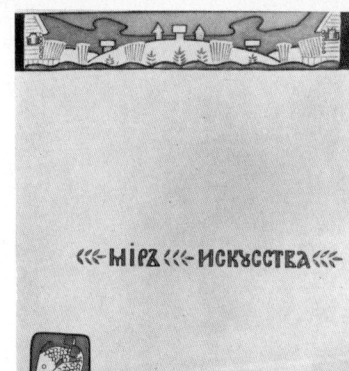

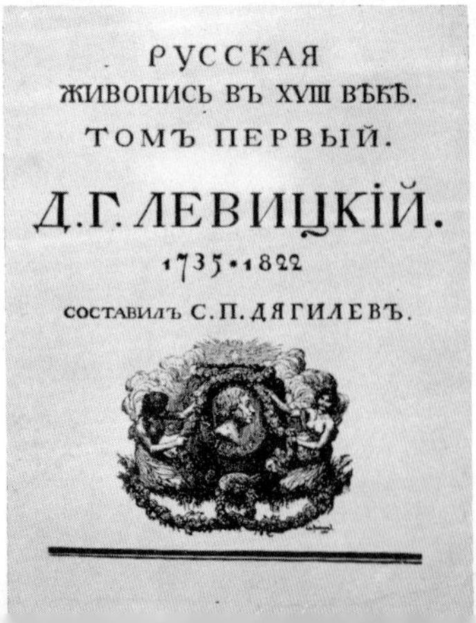

РУССКАЯ
ЖИВОПИСЬ ВЪ XVIII ВѢКѢ.
ТОМЪ ПЕРВЫЙ.
Д.Г. ЛЕВИЦКІЙ.
1735 • 1822
СОСТАВИЛЪ С. П. ДЯГИЛЕВЪ.

The title-page of Diaghilev's only book, a monograph on the eighteenth-century painter Levitsky which revealed Diaghilev as a painstaking scholar. St Petersburg, 1901.

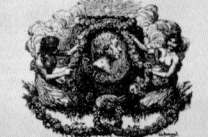

Fokine in the Polovtsian dances from *Prince Igor*. It was this ballet that Fokine considered his greatest choreographic achievement.

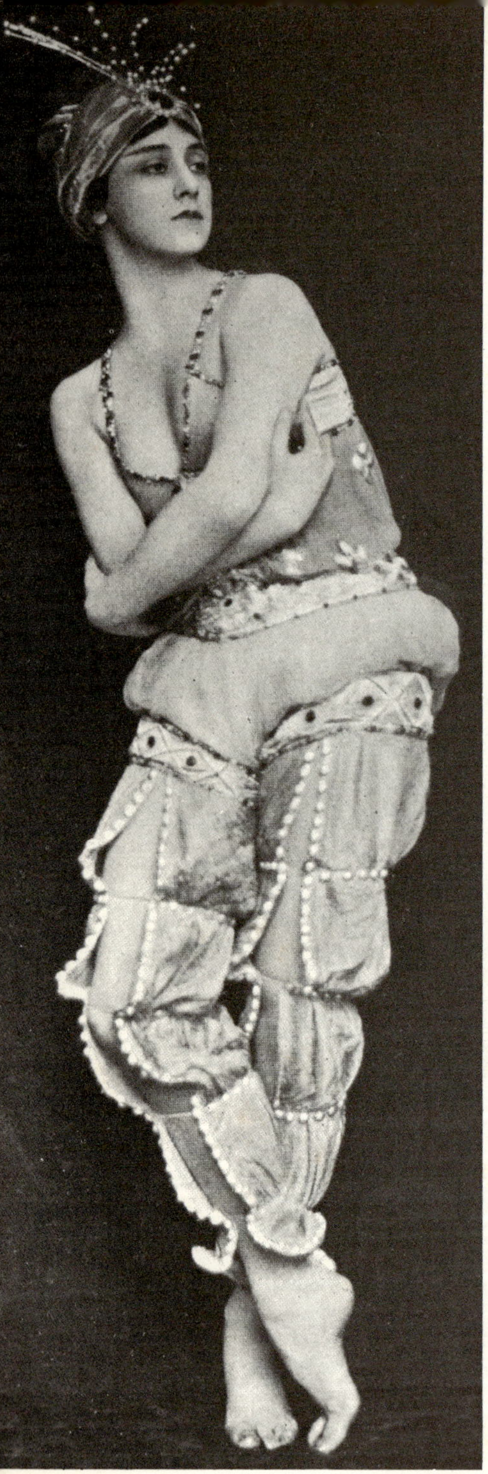

BAKST
1910

BAKST
1910
oiseau de feu

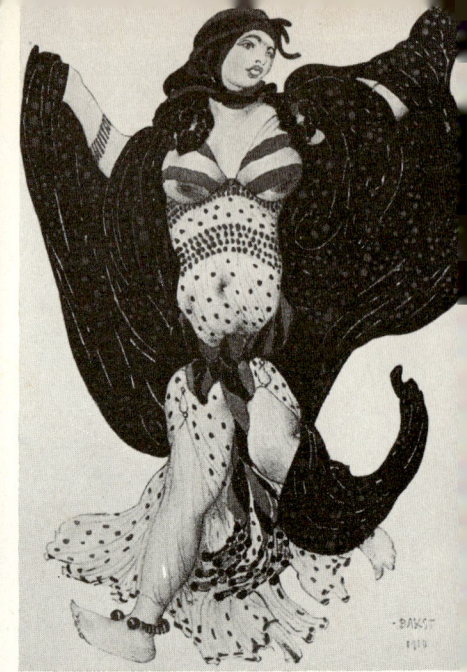

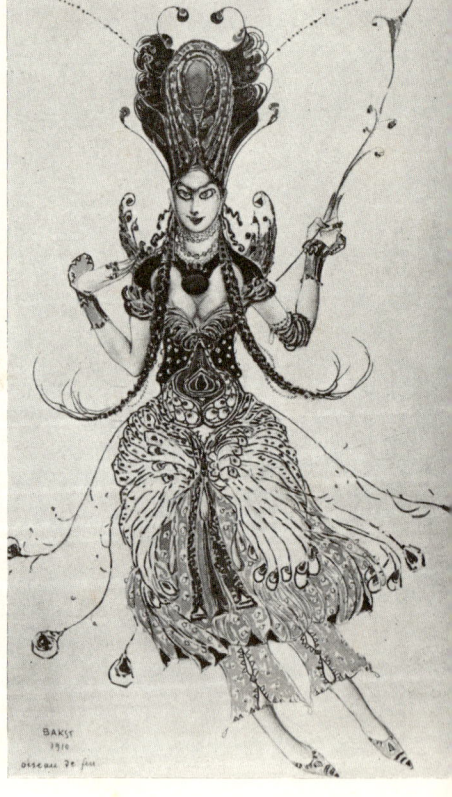

opposite

left Tamara Karsavina in *Schéhérazade*, Covent Garden, 1911. Karsavina created most of the great roles of the Fokine period and also the Miller's wife in *Le Tricorne*. She may rightly be called the first modern ballerina.

above right Costume by Bakst for *Schéhérazade*, which set an oriental fashion in dress designing and furnishing, and had a permanent influence on colour in décor.

below right Sketch for a costume for *The Firebird*, Léon Bakst, 1910. The décor and costumes were, however, finally entrusted to Golovin.

Programme by Bakst for the Paris season of 1911, showing Nijinsky in *La Péri*.

'Study of the dancer in the ballet', 1911, by Marc Chagall, showing Nijinsky in *Spectre de la Rose*.

He was therefore a privileged pupil, if not altogether a satisfactory one. He relied on his friends to see him through his homework, and this characteristic of finding willing collaborators and of pulling strings when necessary remained with him through life. He had a genius for getting out of scrapes.

All his interests were centred on the home, on music-making and the piano, on the prints of famous paintings that decorated the walls and the large folios of reproductions in the library, and especially on the conversation of the many interesting people who visited them. He soon became a proficient pianist, thoroughly at home in reading a score. The Diaghilevs made a special cult of Tchaikovsky, who was a distant family connection. He had dedicated his song 'Is it day?' to Panaieva Kartseva.

Another major influence was his paternal aunt, Anna Pavlovna Filosofova, an outstanding figure of the period, a true Turgenev character. She was both beauty and blue-stocking, a sought-after hostess and an advanced liberal who had played an important role in the reforms of Alexander II, especially in questions of female emancipation. She had even been exiled for a period for giving shelter to the Social Revolutionary terrorist, Vera Zassulich. Although after the Emperor's assassination she moderated her zeal she remained a *frondeuse* to the end. Her husband was a distinguished civil servant, a man of parts but often compromised and always overshadowed by his exuberant wife. The Filosofovs kept open house. Every Wednesday and Sunday there was a big gathering, with places laid for unexpected guests. There they discussed art, politics and society gossip and Diaghilev learned to listen and to sharpen his wits. He and his cousin Dima Filosofov were close friends, though they presented a sharp contrast in character. Dima was a philosopher, calm and retiring, reserved to the point of coldness, keenly intelligent and endowed with a caustic wit. Diaghilev on the other hand was arrogant and highly emotional: an argument with him might often end in blows. It was through Dima that Diaghilev first came to know the small group of artistic revolutionaries whom he was eventually to dominate.

I have stressed Diaghilev's early background because in the west in post-revolutionary days his Russian heritage was forgotten, if it had ever been known. Expatriate though he was, he remained both emotionally and intellectually firmly rooted in Russia. His work cannot be fully understood unless this is realised. One of the declared aims of the original Ballet Russe movement was the patriotic revelation of Russia's artistic achievements to the world. This was never a narrow chauvinism but something far more profound. Diaghilev expressed it as 'the unconscious nationalism of the blood'. It was a sentiment inspired above all by the Russian landscape which, like Tchekov, he so loved in Levitan's painting, and which never seemed far away, even in those impersonal hotel rooms in noisy capital cities.

The Diaghilevs are still remembered by a few old people in Perm, and it is fitting that today the city's Opera House should be a leading experimental centre of Soviet opera and ballet.

3
A Provincial in the Capital Russia 1890/95

In 1890 Diaghilev set out for St Petersburg to study law at the University. It was in no sense a vocation, but a University degree was essential for any career in the civil service. His cousin Dima was abroad at the time and had given him an introduction to his close friends, Walter Nouvel and Alexandre Benois. Walter Nouvel, who was to be Diaghilev's devoted 'attaché' and friend, was a skilled musician whose opinions carried great weight, but he was unambitious and something of a dilettante. A friend describes him at the time as a young man who brought gaiety with him the minute he entered a room, someone of quite exceptional intelligence: 'he sparkled like champagne'. Alexandre Benois, on the other hand, was very far from being a dilettante. He was a skilled painter, a graceful writer and a serious art historian, as well as the leading figure in a group of young people, who jokingly called themselves the 'Neva Pickwickians' and who that very year formed an association known as the World of Art (*Mir Iskusstva*). In addition to Benois, Filosofov and Nouvel, there were L. S. Rosenberg, soon to be known as Léon Bakst, G. F. Kaline, W. V. Skalon; and they gathered around them others of similar interests, among them Charles Birlé, a French diplomat who introduced them to the riches of contemporary art in his country. The group was exceptional in its knowledge and its diversity of interests. It was outward-looking and a trifle blasé, while Diaghilev was still very much the provincial.

Both Nouvel and Benois have described their first impression of Diaghilev. Nouvel says that they found him culturally inferior and treated him with a certain superiority, poking fun at his provincialism. 'He had little general knowledge then, especially of the plastic arts, which did not even seem to interest him.' Benois confirms this, calling him 'a wild and undiscriminating enthusiast, but a man of *flair* from the start.' He was a dandy, where the others, with the exception of Bakst, prided themselves on their picturesque bohemianism, and also something of a snob, which led to constant argument. Again, the 'Pickwickians' were bookworms, but Diaghilev was rarely seen with a book in his hand, though he knew and loved the Russian classics. He seemed to absorb knowledge through conversation and argument.

Later that year, before entering the University, he made his first journey abroad in the company of his cousin Dima. In Vienna he heard his first Wagner opera, *Lohengrin*, and from that moment became an enthusiastic Wagnerian. He also visited Venice, to be so closely associated with him, and Florence, where the impact with the Renaissance was a tremendous and lasting experience. 'In order to judge contemporary art,' he wrote nine years later, 'one must have climbed the peaks of Florentine Art.'

On his return he entered the University. The law bored him, he was uninterested in politics and he cut most of his lectures. It took him six years instead of the customary four to gain his diploma. The World of Art was his true University.

The powerful missionary motive that was to turn a dilettante paper-reading discussion group into a world force came about through the widely differing aims of two groups which had revolted against the all-powerful Academy of Art, and which were in turn influenced by the intensely political climate of the time.

Under the influence of such writers and pamphleteers as Herzen and Aksakov, and mindful of the major role that Turgenev's *A Sportsman's Sketches* had played in the emancipation of the serfs and the social reforms of the 'sixties, most writers of the period felt bound to be politically committed. The painters followed suit, especially as so many of them had been serfs.

On 9 November 1863, thirteen candidates for the Academy's gold medal turned down the set subject, 'Odin in Valhalla', which they considered so remote from actuality as to have no meaning. These thirteen dissidents formed an *artel*, or co-operative, pooling their resources and their profits. They were generously supported by the wealthy Moscow merchant, Pavel Mihailovich Tretiakov, who in 1870 formed The Society of Ambulant Exhibitions, commonly known as 'The Ambulants' (*Peredvijniki*). This, as the name implies, was aimed at decentralising art, bringing it not only to Moscow but to the Russian people as a whole. Its aesthetic had been laid down in 1855 by the radical writer, Nikolai Gavrilovich Tchernichevski in his manifesto, *The Relationship between Art and Reality*, a book that had almost as great an influence as his more famous didactic novel *What is to be done?* It called for realism, for an art which served a social purpose, which was educative above all things. The artist's duty was to teach the illiterate peasant who was beyond the reach of books, either by depicting cruelty and injustice or by showing the ultimate social ideal. To be real, therefore, art had to be committed and it had to be Russian. This meant an end not only to an impersonal international academism, a good thing in itself, but also to the influence of the new French school at the moment of its greatest animation. Repine, the most prominent as well as the most outstanding painter associated with the movement, poured scorn on the works of Delacroix, Degas, Millet and Puvis de Chavannes with a virulence reminiscent of a President of our own Royal Academy. He was indignant at the forty thousand francs realised by Degas' 'Jockeys', 'worth at the most a mere four hundred roubles'. Even the realist *communard* Courbet aroused no sympathetic interest. Surely the chief creative function of academies lies in the rebellions they inspire! Only a few German painters, now forgotten, found any favour. An anthology of this Ambulant painting can be seen today at the Tretiakov gallery in Moscow. It is of considerable importance in understanding Russia.

The movement, all-powerful until 1890, remained a local affair, only Repine's *Volga Boatmen* and more especially Verestchaguine's anti-war paintings becoming known abroad. The

Ambulants had, however, proved that it was possible to revolt against the Academy.

The time was now ripe for a new revolt, this time against both Academy and Ambulants, a revolt that was to be led by the World of Art with Diaghilev as its most progressive spokesman.

For some time, however, he was not conscious of any definite goal. His ambition to become a musician had received a double check. He had gone to show some of his compositions to Rimsky-Korsakov. Even Nouvel, his closest friend, never knew exactly what had occurred at the interview. He certainly suffered a rebuff and is said to have left the room, slamming the door, with the words, 'The future, when I am a celebrity, will show how wrong you are.' True or not, the incident is completely in character. Nor did it spoil the two men's future relationship. Diaghilev had the gift of quarrelling with yet retaining his friends, especially if he had need of their gifts.

The second check was even more drastic. Diaghilev arranged a performance in the presence of friends and acquaintances of a composition based on the Polish scene in Pushkin's *Boris Godounov*. He himself undertook the baritone role of Dmitri. It was a complete failure and he was enough of a realist to accept the verdict. He now entered the second phase of his education, a passionate preoccupation with contemporary painting. He began to find a keen relish in exercising his flair, taking as much interest in the artists themselves as in their work. Unlike many of the St Petersburg intelligentsia, he found himself deeply in sympathy with the Moscow school. The two cities were far apart in their tastes. For example, St Petersburg looked on the icon as something beautiful but as a part of art history, to be studied and classified, while Moscow saw it as a truly native inspiration for the contemporary artist. St Petersburg was interested in the French eighteenth century, Moscow in the post-impressionists. From the start wealthy Muscovite merchants had supported the movement, amassing important collections at a time when the French themselves were still generally hostile or shocked. It was

A Provincial in the Capital

'Diaghilev at the ballet with M. and Mme J. M. S.' (Cocteau)

in Moscow that Diaghilev came under the influence of Sava Mamontov, wealthy merchant and art patron, backer of Stanislavsky and of Russian opera. Instead of making do with the conventional décors of hack artists, Mamontov had enlisted the services of true painters, re-creating *Boris Godounov*, *Khovantchina* and *Sadko* and giving Chaliapin the chance to reveal his genius, a chance that he had not received in the capital. It was at Mamontov's that Diaghilev first met such painters as Serov, Konstantine Korovin, and especially M. A. Vrubel (1856–1910), the most versatile and imaginative artist that Russia has produced. Unfortunately, Vrubel, an artist of genius rather than talent, was to become insane and to die before he could work for Diaghilev. Today he is scarcely known outside Russia.

Moscow led Diaghilev to Paris and to his second European journey. He began to form a collection, although his purchases of Bartels, Dagnan-Bouveret, Israels, Zorn, Liebermann and Puvis de Chavannes seem unadventuresome today. For a time he saw himself as the founder of a museum and suggested to Benois, half in jest, that he should become its first curator.

He was now looking about him seriously for an outlet for his vast energy and ambition. He tried his hand at business speculation with some success and one can well imagine him as a Monte Cristo controlling the destinies of millions, but he was never interested enough in acquiring money for its own sake, and the details of business bored him. Later, as we shall see, he might have made a vast fortune by giving the public what it wanted. He was at no time tempted to do so. He could always drive a hard bargain but he never kept accounts of the vast sums of money that passed through his hands. He was indifferent to personal possessions. His home was a hotel bedroom, his property in a cabinet trunk and some suitcases. He gave away the pictures he collected. Only later in life did he cling to his Pushkin collection, not as negotiable property but as a nostalgic attachment to the Russia he had left behind him. Scrupulously honest himself, he had a sneaking regard for charlatans, provided they operated on a big enough scale. 'I like dishonest people,' he once said, 'you do not have to be particular in your dealings with them.'

But big money was needed for the life he wished to lead. Most revealing is a letter he wrote to his stepmother in 1895.

> 'I am firstly a great charlatan, though with *brio*; secondly, a great *charmeur*, thirdly I have *any* amount of cheek, fourthly I am a man with a great quantity of logic but with very few principles; fifthly, I think I have no real gifts. All the same, *I think I have found my true vocation – being a Maecenas*. I have all that is necessary save the money – *mais ça viendra*.'

The scene was set for his emergence as a power in the world in a profession of his own devising, that of a twentieth-century Medici.

4
The World of Art Russia 1899/1904

The start of Diaghilev's new career came with the founding of a magazine, *The World of Art*, to express the ideas of the group in their revolt against both academism and realism. The groundwork had been prepared and the time was ripe. The influence of the magazine, at first in Russia itself and later, indirectly, throughout the world, can hardly be exaggerated.

The artists gathered round *The World of Art* belonged to no definite school, and subscribed to no one theory of painting. Their ideology, if the word can be applied, was the vague 'art-for-art's-sake' of the Yellow Book 'nineties, the belief that the manner in which a work was composed was the important thing, not the message that it conveyed. They were in no sense political, and their opposition to the Ambulants was purely aesthetic. Unlike his cousin Dima, Diaghilev had no fixed philosophy. He played with ideas and was always exceptionally open to anything new. He could then show the most amazing dialectical skill in imposing his point of view, which he might abandon just as rapidly and adroitly. He never took things for granted and allowed no one in his entourage to do so. Perhaps his most important aim was to show Russia to itself and to the rest of the world, and then to show the rest of the world to Russia. He stood for the freedom of the artist as an individual and the evaluation of the art of the past in that light. 'A work of art,' wrote Diaghilev, 'is the intellect of the artist, his soul, his attitude to life and his sensations.'

It seems extraordinary at the present day that such an attitude should not only have caused surprise but even have aroused hostility. Not a single picture reproduced in the magazine was obscure or startling. At first the Impressionists found no place in its pages.

Diaghilev's difficulties from a material point of view were enormous, even after he had found the necessary capital from the wealthy Princess Tenischeva, the first of his backers (so many of whom were women). Russia lagged behind Western Europe in book production. Neither the right type nor the paper existed, the blocks had to be made abroad and it was necessary to spend whole nights showing the printers how to use them.

The editorial board consisted of strong individualists. Nouvel wrote:

'Its composition is as follows: Dima on the right, Bakst and myself on the left, while the president Serioja (Diaghilev) listens to the declarations of the left and upholds the right. Korovin and Serov are of the left, but they are not often there. While the left holds the majority, the right is often victorious because it has behind it the public and more especially the publishers. This only makes our discussions more vigorous and heated.'

The first argument centred round a forgotten painter of religious subjects, Victor Vasnetsov (1848–1926) for whom the cousins had a great admiration, much to the disgust of Benois. Though Vasnetsov is rightly forgotten today, the dispute is revealing. Diaghilev's motive may possibly have been a genuine enthusiasm for the painter at the instigation of his mystically inclined cousin; it may also have been caused by the heated opposition and the ever-present urge to impose his will. It shows an interesting aspect of Diaghilev's character, a sentimental attachment to the very things that later he set out to destroy. Diaghilev was both sentimental and an iconoclast, internationally-minded and at the same time intensely Russian. With experience, as he became discriminating in his nostalgia for the Russian past, his sentimentality was to be tamed.

It was inevitable that the review should be labelled decadent by its opponents. Diaghilev dealt with this in his first article, writing that decadence implied falling from a height that had never been reached by the previous generation, so that in fact *Mir Iskusstva* must herald an advance. He defined decadence as State art, the mass-production of what had gone before. (This he attacked not only in print but later on in practice when he was urged to reproduce his own early successes.) He went on to underline an article of faith that he was to abide by till the end:

> 'One of the greatest merits of our times is to recognise individuality under every guise and at every epoch ... The desire to make a science out of criticism will never solve the importance of the relative merits of talent. One must sing art, *hail every new manifestation triumphantly.*'

All the collaborators had one aim in common, the praise of subjective, self-revelatory criticism that not only guided the public but also 'the groping and bewildered artist'. It is here that Diaghilev showed his strength, and this was to be his true mission. *Mir Iskusstva* also dealt with music and literature, praising the work of Scriabin and Rachmaninov and introducing to the Russian public César Franck, Debussy, Ravel, Vincent d'Indy and Richard Strauss. Diaghilev himself wrote a number of articles on the theatre and the opera. There is little mention of ballet, except for an occasional violent attack on the feeble décors and the insipidity of the productions of such 'pearls' as *Giselle*, *Sylvia*, *Coppélia* and *La Fille Mal Gardée*. There is as yet no indication of the lines he would follow. His interest had still to be aroused.

One of the most important functions of the World of Art was the organisation of exhibitions. It was in the third exhibition that Diaghilev first revealed his great gifts as a showman. The fact that it was held in the enemy's camp, the Académie des Beaux Arts, was a victory in itself. But this did not satisfy the perfectionist. With the aid of carpenters from the Imperial Theatres he covered the over-ornate walls and split up the large halls with wooden partitions, making a series of small well-lit rooms. This interference with a hallowed institution caused something of a scandal, but the exhibition itself was a success that greatly added to Diaghilev's prestige, and through it he gained a powerful patron in the Grand Duke Vladimir.

The by-products of the World of Art were many, as in time it split into small groups. It led to the founding of a new review, *The Art Treasures of Russia*, edited by Benois, to the *Sources de la Musique Contemporaine*, founded by Nouvel and Nurok, and to the Assemblées Religieuses et Philosophiques with their own review, *The New Path*, as a platform for Filosofov and Merejkovski. Diaghilev was completely uninterested in this last, but the first two activities caused him considerable anxiety. He was fiercely possessive both of friends and ideas. He was reassured when he learnt that Benois' new enterprise would only deal with ancient art and would not interfere with their collaboration. The reason for Diaghilev's omission from the musical group is particularly interesting. Nouvel says that they were frightened of Diaghilev's dominating personality. Angry at first, he readily accepted the explanation that their work was to be on a modest scale whilst it was understood that he cared only for big enterprises.

Filosofov left the Diaghilev entourage around this time. It was to be the end of a fifteen years' friendship that had played a major role in his education. Benois' influence now became paramount. In spite of a subsidy from the Emperor, *Mir Iskusstva* closed down in 1905. It had served its purpose.

5
First contacts with the Ballet Russia 1899

In 1899, Prince Serge Volkonsky was appointed director of The Imperial Theatres in succession to his uncle Ivan Vsevolojsky, who had done great things in his time, notably designing the first productions of *The Sleeping Beauty* and *Casse Noisette*, but who was no longer receptive to new ideas, especially where décor was concerned. Volkonsky was young and energetic and a real man of the theatre. He had earned a considerable reputation as an amateur actor. His education had taken very much the same direction as that of the 'Pickwickians'; he was on friendly terms with them, and the appointment filled them with a hope that seemed to be justified when he took Diaghilev into the service of the theatres 'for special duties'. Diaghilev was in a strong position not only as editor of *The World of Art* but as a favourite of Mathilde Kchessinska, the all-powerful *prima ballerina assoluta* and close friend of the Emperor. His first task was the editorship of the *Theatre Annual*, usually a factual record of productions. The press treated this appointment with considerable hostility, but Diaghilev rose to the challenge. His issue of the *Annual* was a magnificent art edition embellished with vignettes and full-page reproductions and with many articles of permanent value. It cost over twice the sum that had been budgeted. Volkonsky was delighted with the many artists that he met through Diaghilev but he felt that sooner or later there must be trouble. Already his own modest reforms had met with hostility. He wrote: 'If I was an *enfant terrible* in my management of the theatre, and in my desire for reform, Diaghilev was a raging lion. He had a genius for making enemies, but I felt that the artistic results he obtained would excuse his arrogance and lack of tact.'

It was not long before the dreaded incident occurred. Diaghilev, and Benois in particular, had always been interested in Delibes' *Sylvia*. Volkonsky sent out an order entrusting the new production to them. The immediate opposition was so fierce that the order was countermanded even before it reached the printers. This is Volkonsky's version; Benois claimed that the designs were already far advanced. In any case, Volkonsky was not a strong man and was too unsure of his own position to fight for a subordinate. Diaghilev promptly resigned as editor of the *Annual* and immediately a number of artists wrote in to say that they would no longer collaborate. This infuriated Volkonsky though Diaghilev maintained from the first that they had acted on their own initiative. The weak man became stubborn and demanded Diaghilev's resignation from the service. He refused and soon the whole court was involved, right up to the Emperor himself. Finally Diaghilev was dismissed under a harsh law that made it impossible for him to be employed again in any post in the civil service. The unfortunate Volkonsky was forced to resign a few weeks later after a dispute with Kchessinska.

It is possible that if Volkonsky had been a man of another calibre Diaghilev might have carried out his great reforms inside Russia itself. Possible, but highly unlikely. Diaghilev was not the man to work under a committee, nor to stick to a budget, however generous. Moreover like Peter the Great, his hero with whom he sometimes claimed kinship, he was westward-looking and Paris was the great challenge. In effect the Volkonsky episode brought him closer to the cradle of ballet, as well as arousing his interest and introducing him to many of his future colleagues.

We have already seen that *Mir Iskusstva* was not particularly interested in ballet and that Diaghilev himself was far from being a balletomane. It was Benois and to a certain extent Nouvel who saw the possibilities of the art. Ballet in Russia had broken away from the decadence of the post-*Giselle* romantic movement and had never banished the male dancer, but towards the end of

A pencil sketch of Isadora Duncan by Léon Bakst

Petipa's long reign it too had grown stereotyped. The dancers had developed mannerisms, and the balletomanes, carried away by their love of technique for its own sake, eyes glued to opera-glasses, eagerly counted the ballerina's *fouettés*. The décors, commissioned from theatre craftsmen, were such meaningless copies of copies that the girls in the back row of the corps de ballet were always called 'those near the fountain'. The music, except for Tchaikovsky's, was made to measure, with a waltz inserted every twenty minutes for safety. The ballerina often put in a piece of her own choice. No matter if the Czardas found its way to Spain. Volkonsky describes a production of *Tannhäuser*: 'The dances in the first act, the bacchanal in the Venus grotto, had been staged by the great Petipa himself. It was just tip-toe, tip-toe the whole time. The nymphs were ballet dancers, never forgot it themselves and never allowed the audience to forget it.' The more progressive elements had little opportunity of expressing themselves in this stronghold of reaction.

It was the Italian dancer Virginia Zucchi who, in 1885, first turned the young Benois' attention to ballet. He saw her in such ballets as *Brahma* and *Pharaoh's Daughter*, full of the customary absurdities, but the ballerina herself was so real and moving in her expression that he felt that ballet could become a living art. He went night after night, even preparing designs in his puppet theatre for a Zucchi ballet.

A later and even stronger influence that reached Diaghilev himself was the first appearance in Russia, in 1905, of Isadora Duncan. It was not her technique – she had none – nor her conduct, which was outrageous, but her use of classical music and her freedom from the short lampshade *tutu* that entranced them. Benois writes of her 'inner sense of music', though he found her 'lacking in sex appeal and ridiculous at times'. She came upon the scene at exactly the right time to influence a school that she disapproved of profoundly.

Diaghilev was now four years away from his great mission. His education was almost complete, but it remained for him to crown

The scene at the fair in *Petrouchka*, by Benois, 1911. The admiralty spire of St Petersburg can be seen in the background.

Costume design by Benois for *Petrouchka*.

Karsavina in *Petrouchka*, 1911.

top Costume design by Bakst for a *bayadère* in *Le Dieu Bleu*, 1912.

bottom Karsavina in the same production.

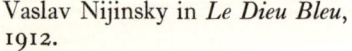

Vaslav Nijinsky in *Le Dieu Bleu*, 1912.

Maquette for the second act of *Daphnis and C[hloé]*. Watercolour by Bakst, 1912.

Michael Fokine, from the drawing by V. Serov, 1912.

opposite Bronze statuette of Nijinsky by Rodin, who warmly defended the choreography of *L'Après Midi d'un Faune* (1912) against attacks by the *Figaro*.

Poster design for the Russian season at the Théâtre des Champs-Elysées, Paris, 1913. A watercolour design by Theodor Feodovsky for a boyar costume in the opera *Khovantchina*.

First Contacts with the Ballet 49

his first career, one that would in itself have assured him of an honoured place in the history of Russian art. This superb climax greatly adds to our knowledge of the man.

In 1904, an announcement appeared in *The World of Art* that an exhibition of Russian historical portraits, from the year 1705 onwards, would be held in the Palais Tauride under the patronage of HM The Emperor, the profits to be devoted to war orphans and widows. Then followed a distinguished list of patrons and advisers, with Diaghilev named as the organising director. Some critics were surprised that Diaghilev of all people should seem to abandon the present in his discovery of the past. None other than André Levinson, later to chide Diaghilev for his modernism, wrote: 'For a time Diaghilev allowed himself to drift. As usual he treated this obsession with the past on a grand scale.'

He and the other critics were writing too near the event to see the clear picture. Obsession it had to be, and one treated on the grand scale; anything else was impossible for Diaghilev. But decidedly he was not drifting, even if he himself did not as yet clearly see the practical outcome. He had already shown his enthusiasm for the eighteenth century in his only published work, a dry and scholarly monograph on the painter Levitsky, famed for his series of portraits of the pupils of the aristocratic Smolny Institute. This, intended as the first volume in a trilogy, was a pioneer work in Russian art history, greatly concerned with attributions and devoid of any artistic theory or personal bias. The book itself, a handsome and well-illustrated quarto published in a very small edition, is long forgotten, but it testifies that the man of flair was also a painstaking scholar. He was awarded a prize for his research by the Académie des Sciences.

Diaghilev, by far the most nationalistic of his group, had soaked himself in the atmosphere of Russian history; he knew what to look for and where to look. He undertook endless journeys, often huddled freezing in peasants' carts along unmetalled roads, visiting provincial governors, finding treasures hung in the galleries of princely palaces or in stacks in the attics of dilapidated country houses. And his charm was such that he could cajole a cherished family portrait from the most recalcitrant owner. He collected in all some three thousand paintings. Then came the work of classification and the full documentation of each picture.

We have already written of Diaghilev's genius for showmanship. The choice of the Palais Tauride was in itself a masterstroke. This palace, built by Catherine the Great for her favourite Potemkin, was lying neglected. Its architecture made it the perfect setting for the exhibition, and Diaghilev brought it back to life again with the furniture and porcelain of the period. The rare reputation that he gained as scholar and artist made possible the backing that he was later to receive.

The year 1905 marked an epoch in Russian, and consequently in world history, the climax of one chapter and the beginning of the next. Diaghilev had no fixed political convictions. He was a liberal, as were all his friends, possibly more sceptical than they. He warmly welcomed the new constitution, and disapproved of republicanism mainly on emotional and aesthetic grounds. He always applauded change but grumbled loudly at the disturbance it brought to his creature comforts. With the extraordinary instinct of the artist he realised, as few did, even those active in the political arena, the exact significance of the treasures he had gathered under one roof, so many of which were to be destroyed.

His speech at the banquet given in his honour was indeed prophetic, and if we are to understand him and to see that his career was deliberate and not a brilliant improvisation, it deserves quoting in full. (The italics are mine.)

'The honour that you have shown me in today's gathering is as pleasant as it was unexpected. Having heard only yesterday of the projected meeting, I was deeply moved, and I felt that I was not ready to receive such a touching expression of attention for everything that has been achieved.

Every festival is a symbol; in honouring a person at the same time we do honour to his ideas. I do not feel like discussing the justice of our beliefs or the realities for which we have been striving. We are used to thinking ourselves in the right, and only our conviction – that it must be either ourselves or no one – upholds us in this unequal struggle for a truth that is only too obvious.

I want to consider the significance of to-night's gathering from a different point of view. There is no doubt that every tribute is a summing-up of achievement, and every summing-up is an ending. I am far from thinking that to-night's banquet is in any sense the end of the aims for which we have lived up to now. Yet I think you will agree with me that thoughts of summing-up and ending come to one's mind more and more in these days. It is this very thing that has been in my mind the whole time I was working. Don't you feel that this long gallery of portraits of big and small people that I brought to live in the beautiful halls of the Palais Tauride is only a grandiose summing-up of a brilliant, but, alas! dead period of our history? Impregnated as I am with the aesthetic point of view, I am as moved by the theatrical brilliance of the eighteenth century as by the legendary brilliance of the sultans of the eighth century, but these fairy-tales I remember only from childhood. The fertile Dan (a prominent Menshevik), with a note of imperceptible sarcasm, makes us realise that we can no longer believe in the romantic heroism of awe-inspiring helmets and heroic gestures.

I have earned the right to proclaim this loudly, because with the last breath of the summer breezes I ended my long travels across the immensity of Russia. It was immediately after those journeys of discovery that I became convinced that the time to sum up is before us. I saw this not only in the brilliant portraits of those ancestors, so far removed from us in time, but more vividly still from their descendants, who were ending their lives. The end of a period is revealed here, in those gloomy dark palaces, frightening in their dead splendour, and inhabited today by charming people who could no longer stand the strain of bygone pageants. *Here not only people are ending their lives, but pages of history.*

It is this experience that has convinced me that we live in an awe-inspiring period of transition. We are doomed to die to pave the way for the birth of a new culture, which will take from us all that remains of our weary wisdom. This is shown us both by history and by aesthetics. Now that I have followed stage by stage the history of artistic portraiture and cannot be reproached as an artistic radical, I can proclaim boldly, and with conviction, that what I am about to say is right.

We are witnesses of the greatest moment of summing-up in history, in the name of a new and unknown culture, which will be created by us, but which will also sweep us away. For that reason *I raise my glass to the ruined walls of the beautiful palaces as well as to the commandments of a new aesthetic.* The only wish that I, an incorrigible sensualist, can express, is that the forthcoming struggle should not damage the amenities of life, and that the death should be as beautiful and as illuminating as the resurrection.'

From the moment that he sat down that night he was complete. The seemingly capricious stages in his education had been assimilated, he had succeeded in showing Russia to herself. Now he was ready to travel and to show Russia to the west and eventually to reveal the west to itself.

6
The Russian Exhibition Paris 1906

In the spring of 1906 Diaghilev visited Greece, Italy, Germany and France. His whole career showed a remarkable sense of timing. This was exactly the right moment for him to establish himself in France. The Franco-Russian alliance had come into being and both Governments were ready to finance any project that would help to cement the friendship. The Russian Pavilion, splendidly decorated by Korovin in the Paris Exhibition of the previous year, had awoken a new curiosity about Russia, a country known up till then less for its art than for its *tournées des grands ducs* in the expensive hotels, gambling resorts and restaurants. Benois, who had been living in Versailles for the past year, was not only the perfect cicerone but could also help him forget his lost friendship with his cousin Dima, who was then in Paris but whom he now met as a stranger. He was also recovering from a severe blow to his pride. As a reward for his work in organising the Palais Tauride exhibition his patron, the Grand Duke Nicolas Michailovitch, had nominated him for an honorary post at court, that of master of ceremonies, which would not only have greatly appealed to the romantic in him but would have humbled his many enemies. The nomination was turned down. This gave a spur to his ambition, and finally convinced him that his career must be made abroad. He put himself in touch with the enthusiastic young organisers of the new Salon d'Automne, men in sympathy with his ideas, and proposed an exhibition of Russian art to be held, on the largest possible scale of course, at the Grand Palais. The idea was accepted with enthusiasm and Diaghilev was placed in full control, with the usual list of

Sketch by Cocteau of Diaghilev and Bakst

distinguished patrons under the presidency of the Grand Duke Vladimir, M. Nelidov, the Russian Ambassador, and others, including the inevitable Comtesse de Greffulhe. She relates how at first she had taken him for a young snob, or worse, for an adventurer, with a highly persuasive manner, and of how he completely won her over by his erudition in discussing her many works of art and especially by his prowess as a pianist who revealed to her a new world of music. On the occasion of that first visit he had laid the solid foundations for all his future activities.

Bakst was placed in charge of decorating the Grand Palais. The sculpture was shown in a formal garden, especially designed with trellis work, and the large collection of icons was given a décor of old gold brocade from which priests' chasubles were made. The exhibition took up twelve rooms and contained seven hundred and fifty exhibits from the Imperial Collections, museums and private owners.

Diaghilev's aim, as expressed in the foreword to the catalogue, was to be selective and to carry out the principles he had laid down in his Palais Tauride speech:

The Russian Exhibition

'The aim of this exhibition is not to give a complete and methodical view of Russian art through the ages. To do this would not only present innumerable difficulties, it would be of doubtful value. Many names, once important, have today lost their former glory, some for the time being, others forever. Many artists to whom their contemporaries attached an exaggerated importance seem to us now completely devoid of merit, *their influence on modern painting being non-existent* . . . These painters offered a distorted view of the nature and importance of Russia's national art of which the present exhibition aims to show the development *through modern eyes* . . . This exhibition represents a faithful image of all those who have had a direct influence on the present-day thinking of our country. *It is an accurate image of the artistic Russia of today with its enthusiastic spirit of research, its respectful admiration for the past and its burning faith in the future.*'

This foreword, in which I have italicised certain key conceptions, is vital to an understanding of Diaghilev's work, often misunderstood at the time by many of the foremost critics, who could not reconcile the juxtaposition of Satie and Tchaikovsky, Petipa and Massine, Bakst and Picasso. Diaghilev had made a choice based on a deliberate aesthetic aim, but in a very real sense the choice had been made long before in his work with the World of Art. Many of those painters, academics and Ambulants, 'to whom their contemporaries attached an exaggerated importance', had been eliminated from the scene by Diaghilev himself and his colleagues.

Even if Russian art – and the art of that period is still greatly underrated – could not challenge comparison with the French genius, except as a springboard for theatrical décors and book-illustration, now for the first time, in the words of the French art-historian, Louis Réau, 'Russia could export new forms of art and send abroad artists who no longer came as pupils but as initiators who could give lessons.'

7
Diaghilev and Fokine Russia and Paris 1909/13

We have left Diaghilev, inspired by the enthusiasm of Astruc, committed to a season of Russian Ballet in Paris, the logical sequel to his season of painting and music. From now on it becomes increasingly difficult to understand Diaghilev's role, if we trace it in isolation and lose sight of the man associated with the World of Art. Ballet is an ephemeral art; the ballet medium demands a number of equal collaborators, out of whose discussions and conflicts something positive will emerge, a work signed by many names. Originally, the name of Diaghilev does not figure on the posters nor in the attributions in the programme under the name of any particular ballet. Only in later years is it used, as a safeguard against imitations. His artistic collaborators, unknown at first, will grow famous within a season or two. They will dispute the honours among themselves, but in most cases they will have forgotten the magician who discovered and launched them. And it is not merely a question of ingratitude, but of complete ignorance that there ever was a magician in the first place to bring them together and blend their ideas, even when he did not originate them. But the dancers at least always knew. It was for Diaghilev that they danced and during his rare absences there was a noticeable fall in the level of performance. The proof of this is clearly shown today, when although ballet has a larger public than ever before and the actual level of dancing has advanced, the art exists in a glorious isolation that has no influence on painting, music or the theatre. It can still enchant the balletomane, but a first night no longer shocks the intellectual into a heated discussion, giving a new vision to a whole generation. In

Diaghilev and Fokine 57

an interview Diaghilev compared himself to a barman who had invented a recipe for cocktails. The recipe has been lost with him. For his first Paris season, Diaghilev had to rely largely on already existing works, carefully selected and modified. The whole venture would have been impossible without the master, Michael Fokine, who was to make a real advance in choreography, bringing Noverre's dicta, Stanislavsky's realism and Duncan's musical ideas to their logical conclusion. At the same time it must be remembered that his most brilliant period lay in the few years, from 1910 to 1914, when Diaghilev was by his side. Many of these works survive today when his later works have been forgotten.

Fokine graduated from the St Petersburg Imperial School at a time when Petipa's rule was absolute and his vast talent unimpaired. Fokine greatly admired him and was encouraged by the master. From the time of his graduation he was interested in every aspect of the art, raising disturbing fundamental questions. Was the ballet in its present form as it should be? Could the ballet be a serious and essential art form for a wide public, or was it destined to remain just a shallow form of amusement?

These queries were parallel to the World of Art's constructive thinking. They received little sympathy from the majority of the dancers and aroused active hostility among officials and balletomanes. This isolation drove Fokine to study painting, music and drama and to spend his vacations in long solitary travels, discovering architecture, peasant dances and costumes and especially the great picture galleries. He was thrown together with many political *émigrés*, among them Kropotkin, Bakunin and Bebel and, although their preoccupations were far removed from ballet, their ideals had a strong influence on his outlook, especially in his wish to 'lead ballet away from the narrow circle of balletomanes and its situation as a court entertainment'. He played the balalaika and danced in factories for the workers and for a time was very much influenced by Tolstoy's views on art.

A teaching appointment at the Imperial School – he began with the junior girls and later graduated to more senior teaching – gave him some influence and the opportunity to learn, and he also began to meet with success as a dancer, enjoying in particular the works of Tchaikovsky and Glazounov. He was receiving the perfect education for choreography at a time when such an education did not exist. Alas, it still is very much a haphazard affair. 'I became a ballet master unexpectedly,' he writes. His first work, in 1905, designed to show off his pupils, was *Acis and Galatea*, considerably modified by official pressure from his original conception. It was a success that led to a number of school and charity performances and received the accolade from Petipa, a card with the words, 'Dear colleague, I am delighted with your composition.' This did not diminish the rage of the die-hard critics, defenders of Petipa against the new destructive element. They were angered in particular by Fokine's insistence on producing a barefoot ballet, forbidden by the rules of the theatre. A compromise was found by painting toes on the feet of the tights!

Fokine's three most important pre-Diaghilev ballets were *Chopiniana*, in two versions (1907 and 1908), *Le Pavillon d'Armide* (1907), and *Egyptian Nights* (1908).

It was *Le Pavillon d'Armide* that first brought Alexandre Benois into touch with Fokine. The original idea came from a suite by Tcherepnin that Fokine had heard at a concert. This resulted in a small ballet, *The Animated Tapestry*, put on at a school performance. The theatre had purchased Benois' libretto for a full-length ballet and this was now commissioned. The trouble that ensued before the ballet was finally produced bound the two men together and made them think of work outside official circles. Fokine was introduced to Benois' friends and they began to hold meetings to discuss the relationship between painting, music and the dance – a startling innovation. According to Fokine the idea of taking ballet to Western Europe was entirely Benois', and Diaghilev was only brought in later. This may possibly have been the case and it is confirmed by Serge Grigoriev, usually infallible on matters of fact. However, he was not present at the

Astruc-Diaghilev meeting which may well have been the decisive factor.

Fokine had already come across Diaghilev during the latter's engagement at the Maryinsky and had looked upon him as 'just another interfering official'. Now at Benois' invitation they came together to discuss a plan of campaign. Diaghilev's successful ventures and his charm had completely changed Fokine's point of view.

The opportunity was there: Astruc's strong financial backing, the patronage of the Grand Duke Vladimir and the long vacation of the Imperial Ballet companies which made possible the engagement of the dancers.

From the start Diaghilev worked with an informal committee *selected by himself*, gathering ideas and throwing out suggestions. The first and most obvious choice was *Le Pavillon d'Armide*, already a proven success. Two more ballets were needed to make up the repertoire. *Chopiniana* was one, renamed *Les Sylphides* by Diaghilev as a tribute to Taglioni and the romantic movement. Benois designed the still famous setting of the ruined moonlit abbey. The third ballet proposed was *Egyptian Nights*. Here Diaghilev intervened more actively to suggest what was almost a new work. A change of title, to *Cléopatre*, led on to a musical upheaval that augmented a re-orchestrated Arensky with music by Rimsky-Korsakov, Glazounov and Tcherepnin. The result was in Nouvel's words 'an abominable salade russe', but with the scenery entrusted to Bakst it became magnificent theatre, especially the sensational entrance of Cleopatra herself, unwrapped by slaves from yards and yards of mummy-cloth. The operas to be given during the season were Rimsky-Korsakov's *Maid of Pskov* (renamed *Ivan The Terrible*), Borodin's *Prince Igor*, Glinka's *Russlan and Ludmila*, Serov's *Judith* and Moussorgsky's *Boris Godounov*. The artists chosen were the best from the Petersburg and Moscow theatres, with one outsider, Ida Rubinstein, a private pupil of Fokine's.

Diaghilev left for Paris to make the final arrangements. During his absence there was a catastrophe. His all-powerful patron, the Grand Duke Vladimir, died and his enemies gained the upper hand. Kchessinska withdrew from the cast and the Imperial subsidy was lost. The money was soon made good however by Misia Sert and Diaghilev's Paris friends. This entailed some notable consequences. The programme was modified, the opera section being drastically cut to *Ivan The Terrible* and one act apiece from *Russlan and Ludmila* and *Prince Igor*, thus putting the whole accent on ballet and convincing Diaghilev that his future lay in France instead of Russia. It was necessary to add one more ballet to the repertoire. This consisted of a *divertissement* under the name *Le Festin*, chosen by Diaghilev from the classical repertoire. One of the items was the famous *pas de deux*, 'The Princess and the Blue Bird' from *The Sleeping Beauty*, renamed as *The Firebird*. Fokine states that Diaghilev had already planned the ballet of that name and had commissioned the music from Liadov. When it was not forthcoming he was left with the name. Had he not claimed to be something of a charlatan? *Le Festin* also gave Diaghilev the opportunity of introducing his favourite Tchaikovsky into the programme with the music of the finale of the second symphony. The critics had denied that Tchaikovsky's music was characteristically Russian and Diaghilev deliberately set out to prove them wrong. He failed to do this during his lifetime. The one act of *Prince Igor* produced a choreographic masterpiece, *The Polovtsian Dances*, created at short notice by Fokine.

Today this does not read like a very revolutionary programme. Diaghilev was improvising, giving the public what he thought it wanted and at the same time showing his skill in what we nowadays would call public relations. Yet, compared with anything the Paris public had seen, it was a startling programme.

The Diaghilev touch was also shown in the preparation of the theatre itself – the old and unfashionable Châtelet, which was usually given over to melodrama on a grand scale. He redecorated and recarpeted the whole house, tearing out seats to make boxes and with the enthusiastic help of Astruc making the foyers and circle into a garden: hence the word *corbeille* for the finest seats. Astruc even saw to it that his first-night audience was decorative, offering seats in the grand tier to 'the most beautiful actresses in Paris . . . Fifty-two accepted . . . I took the greatest care to alternate blondes and brunettes.' A poster was designed by Serov and an illustrated brochure commissioned from a young poet-painter, Jean Cocteau, to be associated with Diaghilev throughout his career.

Nothing had been left to chance, save, in a sense, the first programme. Yet the impact of that programme on the most sophisticated audience in the world is a part of art history, omitted in no memoir of the period. The Comtesse de Noailles summed it up in a phrase: 'Il semblait que la création du monde ajoutait quelque chose à son septième jour.' Writers praised the dancers in an extravagance of language not heard since that day. Pavlova was 'to the dance what a Racine was to poetry, a Poussin to painting, a Gluck to music'; Nijinsky, 'an angel, a genius, a divine dancer who captures our heart, filling us with love'; Karsavina, 'everything about her is poetry . . . You have understood, you, the most exquisite daughter of classical choreography, that a marriage between tradition and an artistic revolution is possible.'

At the first season it was the vigorous male dancers, led by the Polovtsian chief, Adolf Bolm, who made the most rapid conquest. Western Europe had seen no such male dancers since Théophile Gautier, high priest of ballet romanticism, had so summarily banished them from the scene. And they have not been forgotten as the press-cuttings curl and fade. Nor was their work finished with them, though its influence on the dance is intangible.

What was important in the history of art was the effect of the whole. 'All artists understood that this was more than exotic entertainment,' wrote Maurice Brillant. 'That superb dictator, Diaghilev, with no warning, stirred them into action. I do not believe that in the entire history of our theatre there was a more rapid revolution, a more irresistible foreign invasion, or a quicker triumph. The battle, if there was a battle at all, was won on the first night.'

The critics failed to notice the choreography. (At that time, people in the west thought in terms of 'dance arrangement' rather than choreography.) When they wrote, though, they praised the Russian achievement collectively, as 'the triumph of Unity'.

The press was silent about Diaghilev himself. He was too self-assured to relish public applause, and the small group of people who created public opinion and whom he respected understood his achievement to the full. He rejoiced in particular at the success of Nijinsky. Their close friendship was just beginning.

It is essential here to mention this aspect of Diaghilev's life, even though this is not a biography but a study of his influence on the art and thought of his time. It is far more than a private concern. Diaghilev, always surrounded by people, was essentially a lonely man. His closest friend, Misia Sert, was a woman and he had many women friends on whom he relied for support and sympathy, but for reasons beyond the scope of this study he could find no satisfaction in the physical love of a woman. He was continually in search of a male companion, someone exceptional whom he could educate, with whom he could share his artistic ideals and who would be creative. He had no use at all for the pretty boy; he abhorred the effeminate dancer, and the reinstatement of the male dancer to the importance of a Vestris is largely due to him. Nor was he promiscuous. He longed for a stable and fully creative companionship and his search for the ideal, always to elude him, influenced the whole course of his work, as we shall shortly see in his launching of Nijinsky on a new career.

In spite of the artistic triumph, the financial result was a disaster. 'The box-office takings were astronomic,' says Astruc, 'but Diaghilev in his mania for beauty and perfection had passed all bounds.' The backers increased their cheques but there was still a deficit of sixty thousand francs. That was to be the pattern throughout the twenty years of his reign. He would never modify

Diaghilev and Fokine

his plans nor settle for the second best, but somehow at the eleventh hour the money was always found.

It was with the second season, held at the Opéra, that brilliant improvisation gave way to genuine creative work. Each ballet made its powerful impact, giving a new dimension not only to ballet itself but to the separate arts that composed it.

The most sensational item in the second programme was *Schéhérazade*, set to the first, second and fourth movements of Rimsky-Korsakov's symphonic poem. The question of who was responsible for the idea and its treatment was to be hotly disputed, but the vivid impact that created the Ballet Russe style, bringing it from the salons of the wealthy intelligentsia to the *ateliers de mode* and shop windows, is certainly due to Léon Bakst. At curtain-rise the house burst into applause. No one had ever seen such a daring combination of macaw-feather colouring. The Russian painters were not afraid of bold primary colours; theirs was a simplicity in the grand manner, banishing the

Bakst with a dancer at rehearsal (Cocteau)

niggling detail that had been prevalent until then, stimulating the imagination where before there had been naturalistic precision. Diaghilev always insisted on the distinction between naturalism and realism within a given medium which is still so important in contemporary Soviet criticism.

The exoticism of the Ballet Russe was soon taken up by the grands couturiers, led by Paul Poiret; oriental balls became the rage; and the Russian influence could be felt in poster-design and interior decoration. For the first time, too, a choreographer had been directly influenced in his use of movement by a painter, though Fokine would never acknowledge this. Throughout the Diaghilev period the painter's role grew in importance. He no longer decorated, framed or embellished a finished work. *Schéhérazade* was also a choreographic innovation. A complex narrative was told in dance alone, abandoning the conventional mime that so greatly inhibited dramatic realism. Its ground pattern, as in all Fokine's works, was masterly.

It is difficult for anyone who has only seen it in a revival to realise the vast importance of the work. The very speed of its success and the imitations it in pired made it hackneyed, though to the general public it remainesd a favourite and in difficult time Diaghilev could have lived on its proceeds. He realised with great shrewdness that as memory brightened every colour, it would seem drab unless the colours were intensified, and that was impossible. Moreover, unlike most Fokine ballets, it had been inspired by his dancers, by the contrast between the tall and stately Rubinstein and the pantherine Nijinsky. When finally under great pressure it was revived, Diaghilev greeted it with such gusts of laughter that he broke his chair.

The next ballet, also designed by Bakst, was a striking contrast. *Carnaval*, to Schumann's music, had originally been put on at a charity ball and was afterwards taken over by the Maryinsky. Diaghilev was at first hostile to what was essentially an intimate work but, when finally persuaded, he stressed the intimacy by substituting for the garden set an interior beautifully

left Costume design and *below* maquette by Goncharova for the production of *Le Coq d'Or*, Rimsky Korsakov's opera, danced and mimed by the ballet with singers in the wings. Paris, 1914.

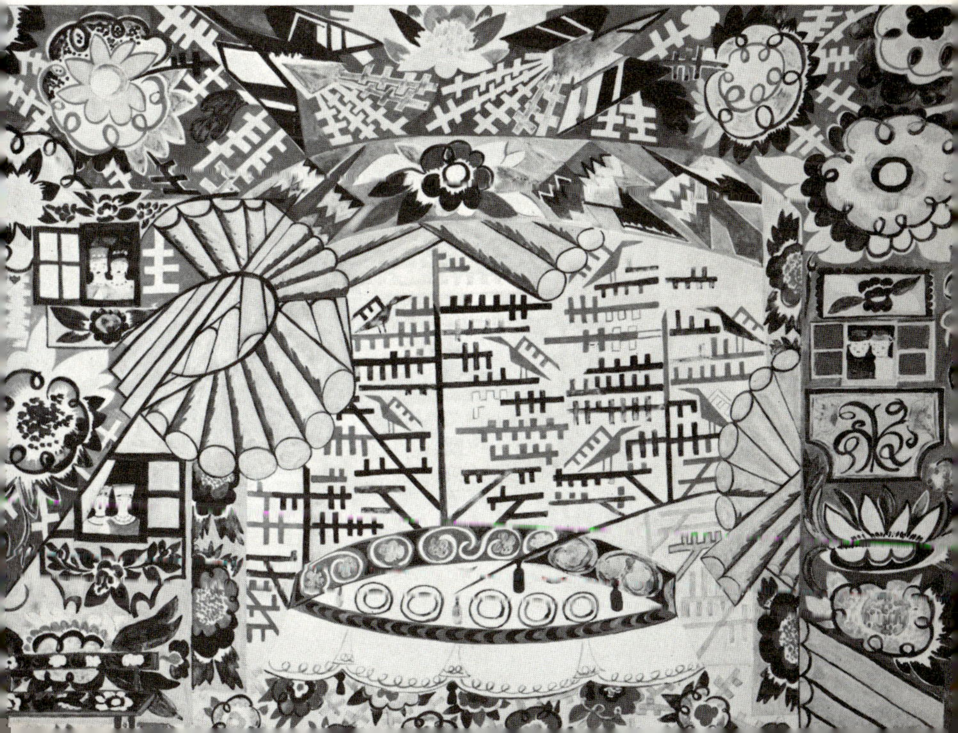

Design by Benois for Stravinsky's *Le Rossignol*, 1914; this was revived in 1920 with décors by Henri Matisse.

Costume design for *Le Soleil de Nuit* by Larionov, 1915. This was the first ballet with choreography by Massine, and was given as a Red Cross Gala performance.

top Maquette for the scenery of *Contes Russes* by Larionov, 1917, and *bottom* a sketch for the drop curtain in the same production.

Alexandre Benois by Bakst.

Sketch done in a café by Larionov in 1917, showing Goncharova, Diaghilev, Massine and Diaghilev's valet.

designed by Bakst. For the first time he risked presenting a dancer who had yet to make a reputation in Russia, Lydia Lopokova. Her Columbine and Nijinsky's astonishing Harlequin saved a subtle work.

The first true creation – all its elements had been specially commissioned – was *The Firebird*. Diaghilev had long wanted to present a characteristic Russian fairy tale, but the project had been delayed by Liadov's dilatoriness. 'I have just bought the ruled paper,' he told Diaghilev when they met two years after the commission. Diaghilev had heard the twenty-seven-year-old Stravinsky's *Fireworks* and *Scherzo Fantastique* at the Concert Ziloti in 1908 and had decided that this was his man, in spite of the scepticism of his 'cabinet', who were greatly concerned about risking a commission from an unknown composer. It was Diaghilev's first major discovery. The two men became friends and collaborated throughout the next twenty years. There were numerous quarrels, but they rarely interfered with the work. Stravinsky was inspired by Diaghilev's enthusiasm and the vision that enabled him to see the finished product after he had heard the first few notes.

Stravinsky and Fokine worked together phrase by phrase in a harmony that had not been known since Tchaikovsky's collaboration with Petipa. Golovin gave the ballet a magnificent setting and costumes.

Stravinsky afterwards expressed himself as not totally satisfied with the choreography, but subsequent versions have shown, as is invariably the case, that Diaghilev's judgment was correct.

One result of the ballet had far-reaching effects. Originally it had been conceived with Pavlova in mind but when she heard the music she found it an 'incomprehensible cacophony'. This may have proved the last straw, since she was already becoming restive at the thought of Nijinsky's growing fame. She left Diaghilev to begin her glorious career as 'a soloist surrounded by a company'. Her influence on the dance has been incalculable but, where the allied arts are concerned, completely non-existent.

Diaghilev with Nijinsky at a rehearsal for *Schéhérazade* (Cocteau)

Her role was taken over by Karsavina, an artist completely in harmony with Diaghilev's aspirations: it could not have been bettered. Diaghilev himself operated the switchboard.

The fourth ballet was a revival of *Giselle*, which Diaghilev had long considered a masterpiece. The Russians had taken it over from the French and had turned a pretty anecdote into a universal drama. Nijinsky had now given the male role of Albrecht an importance that threw the whole ballet into perspective. But for once Diaghilev had failed to gauge the public taste. The colour of Bakst's *Cléopatre* and *Schéhérazade* had made Benois' moonlight seem insipid, while Petipa's period romanticism and Fokine's new romanticism failed to blend. To the Parisian sophisticate *Giselle* belonged to the dust-laden storeroom of the Opéra, to be taken out every now and then and dusted for a popular Sunday matinée. Was it not a part of that very thing these Russians were attempting to destroy?

It was in London that Diaghilev's deep roots in classicism were to bear a rich fruit. In Paris, ironically, for a short time after his death his last great ballerina, Olga Spessivtseva and his last pupil,

Serge Lifar, were to turn *Giselle* into an unforgettable experience.

The year 1911 was a decisive one for Diaghilev; it saw the establishment of his own permanent company, the signing of the important contract with Monte Carlo and the company's London début.

For the first two years the enterprise had been seasonal and temporary, depending on the goodwill of the Imperial Theatres when it came to lending its artists. Diaghilev had too many enemies for this to be a satisfactory arrangement. Moreover it was in his nature to demand absolute authority and not to be confined in the making of contracts to a certain period in the year. His opportunity came by chance, of which he took full advantage. Nijinsky was due to give a performance of *Giselle* at the Maryinsky Theatre in front of the Dowager Empress. He had been warned that his costume was considered inadequate but he refused to change it. The Dowager Empress complained and in spite of an apology Nijinsky was summarily dismissed. This gave Diaghilev the opportunity to employ him the whole year round with, of course, a full company of dancers.

The Monte Carlo contract arrived in time to give him some welcome security. There were only three performances a week; the programme served as a *répétition générale* for Paris and gave the artists time in which to rest. Monte Carlo was also the resort of the rich and influential from all countries, a perfect centre for the personal word-of-mouth propaganda of which Diaghilev was a master, sounding out on occasions the barber or the *maître d'hôtel*. In addition Monte Carlo came to fulfil a far more important function; it was essential to Diaghilev's method of creation from 1911 to his death.

Diaghilev created through others. He prided himself on being 'a collector of geniuses'. He would visit art exhibitions and concerts, meet poets and musicians, contacting those whom he thought useful to his work. He relied on his flair in the first place, but a ballet could not be produced by snap decisions. The various artists must meet together in a relaxed atmosphere, they must talk, produce ideas, tear them to pieces and think again. His painters were easel-artists and they had to get to know the nature of ballet; the composer and the choreographer, with the aid of a piano, had to learn to speak the same language. Monte Carlo was the ideal centre for such work. Every season artists flocked there, often as his guests, and many a ballet was conceived in the Hôtel de Paris, at a supper table presided over by Diaghilev. It was his Versailles. On one occasion at a première in the Monte Carlo Opera House, he told the present writer, 'If the theatre burned down tonight, a large part of the world's creative artists would be wiped out.' And it was true.

The same year brought the company to the Royal Opera House, London, for the Coronation season, sponsored by a devoted and understanding friend, the Marchioness of Ripon. London saw a repetition of the Paris success. 'The repercussion of the Diaghilev ballet on the university youth of Britain,' wrote Jacques Emile Blanche, 'is scarcely credible. The influence of these performances on English intellectuals is incalculable.' The Ballet Russe certainly played a big role in shaping what has been called the Bloomsbury movement, which supported it from the start. There was, however, a difference. The English audience already appreciated great classical dancing, thanks to Adeline Genée and the recent visits of Lydia Kyasht and Anna Pavlova. After that first season Diaghilev stayed longer in London than anywhere else save Monte Carlo. He found a faithful public, one that was too faithful to give him the creative stimulus he so badly needed. Paris was hypercritical, demanding to be shocked into attention every season by some novelty. London loved the ballets it knew and applauded its favourite dancers the moment the curtain rose. Diaghilev always preferred to stake everything on a novelty rather than sit back and cash in on past successes.

London was to give him only a few collaborators: Sacheverell Sitwell, Lord Berners, Constant Lambert, and Edwin Evans as musical adviser. But it was to provide him with many outstanding dancers carefully disguised under foreign names: Sokolova, de Valois, Markova, Dolin, Savina. As we shall see, in one respect his influence in England was greater and more enduring than anywhere else. In his second London season later the same year Diaghilev presented a dazzling pride of ballerinas, headed by Pavlova, Karsavina and his old enemy, la Kchessinska – 'un adversaire bien digne de moi', as he once said to the writer. She danced *Swan Lake* with Mischa Elman, the violinist idol of the

An impression by Cocteau of the scene in the wings at the end of *Spectre de la Rose*

period, playing the *adagio*, one of the great and extravagant gestures so typical of the man.

The year 1911 also represents the climax of the first phase of Diaghilev's career, with the triumph of the Stravinsky–Benois–Fokine *Petrouchka*, still the greatest of all dance dramas, and *Le Spectre de la Rose*, the ballet *à deux* that was the zenith of the partnership of Karsavina and Nijinsky, whose leap through the moonlit window turned his name into a household word and earned considerable sums for his dresser, who sold rose-petals from his costume to wealthy admirers. The libretto for the ballet had been suggested by the French writer Jean Louis Vaudoyer, who had the idea of wedding some verses of a poem by Théophile Gautier to the music of one of his favourite composers, Weber's *Invitation à la Valse*. This was the start of what was finally to become a Franco-Russian artistic venture. It also brought the poet back to ballet, from which he had been missing since the time of Gautier.

The years 1909 to 1911 had firmly established the Ballet Russe movement; it had even accelerated the translation of Russian literature. 'Nous commençons à devenir des gens très bien, à avoir des relations très chic, très pourries, très ballet russe,' said one of the characters in de Flers and Caillavet's brilliant comedy, *Le Bois Sacré*, as early as 1910.

The ballet of these three years was an extension of the World of Art, something truly Russian conceived in Diaghilev's flat in St Petersburg – 'Chancery and Parnassus in two rooms' – with Diaghilev's old nanny presiding over the samovar. The choreographer, Michael Fokine, was fully formed and had developed his own ideas on the dance, though these were modified by Diaghilev and his friends to a degree that he did not realise. A close collaborator says that though he was a choreographer of genius he was singularly lacking in taste, which is certainly borne out by his painting.

In those three seasons there are two other remarkable accomplishments to be noted. From 1910 onwards when people talked of going to the ballet it could only mean the Russian ballet; and this label persisted for many years after Diaghilev's death. Also, for the first time there were a number of motives for a visit: one went for Karsavina and Nijinsky or Fokine's last work, for Bakst's décors, or for Stravinsky's music. The ballet had become a travelling museum. Diaghilev commented that for the modern painter it represented what the fresco had been for the painter of the Renaissance, and that this rapid medium suited the temperament of the Russian artist to perfection. Many of the artists painted the scenery themselves. A critic of this period defined it as 'a magic lantern for grown-ups'. Diaghilev's complete success as an innovator was strikingly revealed in 1911 when the official ballets from the Imperial Theatres gave a Paris season at the Théâtre Sarah Bernhardt. In spite of brilliant dancing it was completely eclipsed.

With the foundation firmly established there would no longer be any purpose in following the fortunes of the company in detailed chronological order. It is important, however, to deal with certain key works and the changes they brought about.

Diaghilev was faced with the problem of renewing himself. He had become absolute dictator of his organisation and felt that he had now exhausted the possibilities of Fokine's neo-romanticism. His ambition was to inspire and educate a choreographer. Vaslav Nijinsky was his obvious choice.

There were four new ballets in 1912. The choreography of three of them was by Fokine: *Le Dieu Bleu*, a Hindu legend by Jean Cocteau with music by Reynaldo Hahn; *Thamar*, with a libretto and décors by Bakst and music by Balakirev, an attempt to re-create the excitement of *Schéhérazade*, the last of the exotics; and Ravel's *Daphnis and Chloë*, commissioned when Diaghilev was in Paris for the historic concert series, which is strong evidence that he was not rushed into the venture by Benois.

Le Dieu Bleu, in spite of Nijinsky's Indian-inspired gestures, failed to interest the Paris public, who had been so impressed by the Siamese dancers at the great exhibition. And *Daphnis and Chloë*, one of the greatest scores written for ballet, presented enormous difficulties for choreographer and dancers. The heated discussions that ensued finally made Diaghilev decide to part with Fokine, and strained his relationship with Ravel. Later he turned down *La Valse*, which the composer had specially written for him, because he thought it lacking in dramatic development. Time has proved him right, but this led to a final break.

8
Successes and scandals

It was the fourth creation of the 1912 season, *Prélude à l'après-midi d'un faune*, with Nijinsky as choreographer and dancer, that announced the new Diaghilev period with a flourish. Igor Stravinsky describes its creation in his autobiography:

'At the suggestion of Bakst who was enthusiastic about archaic Greece this work was to show an animated bas-relief seen in profile. Bakst's role in this ballet was the predominant one. Even without the décor and the beautiful costumes created by him, he indicated the smallest details of the choreography.'

It was decided to use Mallarmé's *Eclogue* for the libretto and to set it to Debussy's music.

Nijinsky was an instinctive choreographer without the knowledge or the discipline to follow the constantly changing aesthetic aims of Diaghilev and his circle. This ten-minute work for eight artists required one hundred and twenty rehearsals.

When the storm broke it was not on aesthetic but on moral grounds, on account of the alleged indecency of the Faun's final onanistic gesture with the nymph's scarf.

'Our readers,' wrote Calmette, editor of the influential *Le Figaro*, 'will be surprised not to find the criticism of my esteemed collaborator Robert Brussel, in its customary position. I have suppressed it.' He went on to write that he was not competent to judge the ballet as a work of art. In any case, 'those who talk of art or poetry in this connection are making fun of us – we were shown a vile and incontinent faun whose gestures revealed an erotic bestiality . . .' And so on for many columns. *Le Temps*, more moderate, agreed that it was a serious mistake, but then the Russian ballet 'had barbaric tendencies'.

The musicians felt, with some reason, that Debussy's score had suffered, but the artists leapt to Diaghilev's defence, headed by Odilon Redon and Rodin, who stated that nothing could be more moving than the final gesture of despair. The affair was discussed at a high diplomatic level and, for fear of police intervention, the ballet could only be given when the final gesture had been eliminated.

Press puritanism is still a commonplace. The ballet had been discussed as much as any play or novel, and it had made people think. To Diaghilev this was a way of life. He had no use for ballet as mere entertainment.

Characteristically in this very year of scandal and novelty he secured his links with tradition by engaging the great Italian maestro, Enrico Cecchetti, to teach his company. Cecchetti was completely out of sympathy with any of Diaghilev's aims, but he

A drawing by Cocteau of Diaghilev and Nijinsky

Successes and scandals 79

was a great pedagogue, whose presence was all the more necessary as the ballet began to fill its repertoire with modern works. Diaghilev's influence in all directions was widespread, sometimes even destructive, but he never questioned the excellence of academic dance-training. He believed it to be the indispensable basis for every type of choreography and that one could express modern ideas as did Picasso and Stravinsky, not in spite of, but through the medium of a classical discipline. He once said:

'I am accused of treating classicism with neglect and contempt. Rubbish. Classicism like everything else evolves. We must first make up our minds as to what is classicism. There were outcries, at first, about the music of Igor Stravinsky – now it is classic.

Life doesn't stand still . . . Even nature seems to change its aspect. Where today will you find the classic landscape of the romantic period, with its willows, its lake, the marble figures and the sluggish clouds?

The lake has been filled in and the trees cut to give way to signals, stations and seats. The physical organism grows old and is destroyed, but art itself must have a permanent youth, change and be renovated.

Classicism is the university of the modern choreographer, but to develop theatrical creation we cannot remain academic. We have all learned algebra and Greek but not in order to solve problems nor to speak Greek. The dancer and ballet master of today must matriculate, just as Picasso must know anatomy and Stravinsky his scales.'

The following year saw a further scandal, on aesthetic grounds this time.

Diaghilev, greatly under the influence of Gauguin's Tahitian paintings, wished to produce a primitive pagan ballet, but one set in Russia.

The painter-archaeologist, Nicolas Roerich, together with Igor Stravinsky, who was to compose the music, had conceived a ballet, *Le Sacre du Printemps*, based on the primitive rites of Russian tribes. There was little narrative though the ballet culminated in the sacrifice of a chosen virgin. It consisted of ensembles rather than the solo dances that the public expected in a ballet. It was harsh, even brutal, marking a complete break from neo-romanticism. The music was so rhythmically complex for the dancers of that period that they compared the rehearsals to arithmetic lessons. The difficulties were increased by Nijinsky's lack of experience and his tentative method of working. To assist him in this work Diaghilev asked Jacques Dalcroze to send him an experienced eurhythmic instructor. This was Marie Rambert, who was to play such a big role in the development of ballet in England.

The curtain had scarcely risen before there was an outburst of stamping and catcalls, the smart first-night audience behaving like hooligans. Fighting actually broke out and the police were called in. The Dowager Countess of Pourtalès, a *grande dame* of great dignity and a patron of the ballet since its inception, shook her fist at Astruc and told him that she was too old to be taken in by such foolishness. Debussy, in the box with Diaghilev, blocked his ears. The critics with few exceptions agreed with the public. It was the same reception that Hugo's *Hernani* had received in 1830, and, as on that occasion, the booing ushered in a new period of art. It remained Diaghilev's proudest achievement. Cocteau has a moving description of a drive in the Bois with Diaghilev, Stravinsky and Nijinsky after the performance, Diaghilev reciting Pushkin with tears in his eyes. For this man, years ahead of his time, *Le Sacre du Printemps* was a great Russian work, rooted in an old tradition which, even if it was rejected now, would be understood in the years to come. It cost Astruc his management of the magnificent new Théâtre des Champs Elysées but he was a big enough man to understand the value of his sacrifice.

The first production was not altogether an artistic success and the ballet was later revived with choreography by Massine. What

Successes and scandals

Cocteau's impression of Stravinsky
playing *Le Sacre du Printemps*

it did was to turn the attention to the primitive at a time when a few *fauves* were beginning to collect African sculpture. It enormously extended the scope of choreography, which had hitherto exploited the weightless. Here the pull of the earth and the dead weight of the body were stressed, inspiring many modern dance movements. Julie Sazonova summed it up when she wrote:

> 'It was necessary to make an end of dance accompanied by music as well as by music interpreted by the dance: it was necessary to create an art which was at the same time plastic and musical, the ideal ballet. The very sense of the music must be expressed in the dance. The last dance of *Le Sacre du Printemps* is perhaps the most striking example: the dancer's body was really shaken by the frenzy of Stravinsky's rhythms.'

The ballet called for a new type of dancer, one more rhythmically aware. It was a paradox that this type of choreography should have been launched by a dancer so famed for his elevation.

Le Sacre du Printemps marks the beginning of Diaghilev's campaign to impose his will upon the public. By doing so he was to facilitate the struggle of painters, musicians and choreographers all over the world. In retrospect he called this hotly debated première, 'le moment de la musique moderne'.

The other Nijinsky ballet of that season, *Jeux* by Debussy, based on a game of lawn tennis, fell flat. It was their last collaboration. Nijinsky's wedding in South America brought about an angry breach and later Nijinsky's tragic mental breakdown made any new association impossible. It is more than possible that Nijinsky as choreographer had contributed all that he had to give. His contribution had been a major one not only in its direct results but in the confidence that it gave to Diaghilev himself as a creator of talent.

The immediate pre-war season brought the temporary return of Fokine, but nothing new artistically. It did, however, introduce Diaghilev to two of his most distinguished future collaborators. The Joseph in Richard Strauss' *La Légende de Joseph* was a young ensemble character dancer from the Bolshoi Theatre, Leonide Massine. He had graduated only two years before but he greatly impressed Diaghilev, who signed him on a long-term contract. His other discovery was the painter Natalia Goncharova, who had studied in the Moscow school of painting and had exhibited with *Mir Iskusstva*. She had followed Diaghilev's career with enthusiasm. A painting that she exhibited at Moscow in 1905, a view of a flower-strewn table in front of a window, has a mask of Diaghilev in the left-hand corner. She showed it to him one night by candlelight before the exhibition opened. He was so delighted that he determined to call on her when the right time came. She designed the scenery and costumes of Rimsky-Korsakov's *Le Coq d'Or* in a sung and danced version, bringing in the inspiration of Russian folk art, not yet hackneyed as it was to become.

This marked a switch from St Petersburg to Moscow, which was in a way more Russian, certainly less sophisticated, and for

Successes and scandals

'Diaghilev, Massine and the gardener's boy' (Drawing by Larionov)

that very reason more forward-looking and more closely in touch with French avant-garde movements.

At the same period Diaghilev met Michael Larionov, of all the Russian painters the one who was most perfectly attuned to his new ideas. Larionov was born in the small town of Tiraspol, the son of the local chemist. He won a scholarship to the Moscow Academy and soon established himself as a rebel. To advertise his new ideas he had gone around Moscow with a brightly-coloured picture painted on his face. This delighted Diaghilev, who promptly sent the young artist to Paris with the exhibition of 1906. There the Fauve movement excited him and he felt completely at home. He was to spend most of his life in Paris. Larionov was interested in every branch of art, in particular the popular arts of the circus and fairground. During his short time in the army he had studied the various means of expression of the Russian soldier, from his songs and dances to his *graffiti*.

Benois was an aristocrat, Bakst a highly sophisticated Jew, Larionov a man of the people bringing with him an entirely fresh point of view. He could follow and at times anticipate Diaghilev, who was able to select from and guide his many exciting ideas. These were so many and so exciting that he was never to receive his due as a painter. He lacked the necessary concentration to advance in any one phase. The constant bustle of the theatre was his true milieu. Larionov was one of the very few of Diaghilev's inner circle to do him full justice.

The war cut Diaghilev off from his original team and his homeland. The continued progress of his work was a miracle of determination, though it was only possible because of the goodwill earned in the five years before 1914. There were times during the war when Diaghilev behaved like a head of state, invoking the aid of the Pope, the King of Spain and President Wilson.

The war found him in Italy, and later in Switzerland, with his company scattered, his future engagements cancelled and his financial situation desperate. He had at the moment only one member of his troupe, the new recruit from Moscow, Leonide Massine, whose astonishing gifts he knew he had to develop, re-creating a company around him.

'A new *maître de ballet* is a great event. I have been singularly lucky in this respect.' Diaghilev was unduly modest here. He had divined Massine's gifts and set out to give him the most intensive training ever received by a choreographer. Cecchetti was there to provide the essential classical groundwork. A new cabinet was formed, with Stravinsky, who was living close by, and Goncharova and Larionov, who were specially summoned. Larionov worked daily with Massine, introducing him in particular to the drawings and engravings of Jacques Callot, a storehouse of choreographic inspiration. Diaghilev took him to museums and announced with real joy: 'He knows things before one explains them.' The faithful Grigoriev, under a bombardment of telegrams from Diaghilev, gathered dancers from Russia and Poland. The offer of an American tour and a substantial advance from Otto Kahn had saved the situation.

A sketch by Pablo Picasso for the backcloth of *The Three-Cornered Hat*, 1919.

Detail for the backdrop by André Derain for *La Boutique Fantasque*, 1919.

left and opposite Designs for *Chout*, 1921, by Larionov. Larionov was the only painter to be entrusted with choreography, and he formed an important link between Russia and the French school.

Costume by Larionov for *Le Renard*, 1922. This ballet was revived in 1929 and marked the début of Lifar as a choreographer.

Costume designs by Bakst for the Alhambra production of *The Sleeping Princess*, 1921. Although this production had tremendous influence in England, its return to classicism was before its time and it proved a financial disaster

Successes and scandals

There was one première in Paris, a charity matinée at the Opéra of Massine's first ballet *Le Soleil de Nuit*, to the music of Rimsky-Korsakov's *Snegourochka* and with settings by Larionov. It was an outstanding success in the new idiom of folklore and burlesque that Massine and Larionov were to follow up in 1917 with *Contes Russes*, with music by Liadov. Although this was the only new work of the one-day Paris season, Diaghilev had been particularly active, experimenting with a ballet designed by Goncharova to be called *Liturgie* and commissioning a further ballet from Stravinsky, *Les Noces*, and one from Prokofiev, *Chout*.

Although Diaghilev found much to admire in America he was delighted when a season was arranged direct with Nijinsky and he could return to his small creative group in Europe.

The Massine period lasted until 1921. It brought with it a great enrichment of choreography, with fresh advances in music and a new vision in décors as exciting as in the early years.

Two of Massine's masterpieces, *Les Femmes de Bonne Humeur* (1917) and *La Boutique Fantasque* (1919), were planned in Italy, where Diaghilev had been making active researches in the musical archives. His first discovery was a score by Scarlatti which he gave to Tommasini to orchestrate. The scenery and costumes were designed by Bakst, who introduced Massine to Longhi and Hogarth. Bakst's genius had not exhausted itself in his pre-war orientalism. Here he conceived the Italian square as seen in a crystal, thus concentrating the action. The subject was taken from a comedy by Goldoni. Massine found a personal style of danced mime that derived from the Italian *Commedia dell'Arte*. The other Italian-inspired ballet, *La Boutique Fantasque*, with music by Respighi based on various pieces by Rossini, had décor by Derain, the first distinguished French easel-painter to work for the ballet. The Russian Ballet was now to become a Franco-Russian collaboration, with Diaghilev as the enthusiastic patron of the post-impressionists.

The most important work of this period was what Diaghilev proudly called one of his 'magnificent failures', *Parade*. It resulted in the biggest scandal since *Le Sacre du Printemps*. It was a collaboration between Cocteau, Satie and Picasso. The simple score was punctuated by sounds from a typewriter and the screeching of sirens. *Musique concrète avant l'heure?* The drop curtain and the set were magnificent simplifications, the colourless cubist-inspired costumes (except for those of the brilliant Chinaman and the blue acrobat) were erected on the dancers rather than worn by them and became animated pieces of scenery. Cocteau guided Massine and dominated the choreography, which was literary rather than visual. The poet Guillaume Apollinaire wrote an apologia for the programme, claiming that this was a new union of painting and the dance and that it was the manifestation of a new spirit 'where reason demands that the arts march together with scientific and industrial progress'.

In that the dance suffered *Parade* deserved to fail, but it was a manifesto which pointed the way for many future theatrical productions and brought Picasso into close contact with Diaghilev. In addition Satie's work was followed up by his disciples Auric, Milhaud, Poulenc and Sauguet. *Parade* came in 1917, and though Diaghilev was non-political the Russian Revolution excited him, influencing his artistic outlook in a totally different direction from that of the revolutionaries themselves. Later he was to be delighted when Mayakovski told him, in the writer's hearing, that his ballets were far too revolutionary to find favour in Russia.

The failure of *Parade* kept him away from Paris for over two years, the critics having condemned him on high moral grounds rather than on aesthetic ones.

Picasso's next ballets, *Le Tricorne* (1919) and *Pulcinella* (1920), for which Diaghilev had found a suite by Pergolesi as a basis for Stravinsky, were both accepted as masterpieces. *Le Tricorne* succeeded more than any ballet since *Petrouchka* in fulfilling the unity between dance and painting that Apollinaire had mistakenly claimed for *Parade*. The folk costumes of Spain were translated for the stage by Picasso, the popular music for the

Successes and scandals

Pablo Picasso and Igor Stravinsky (Cocteau)

symphony orchestra by de Falla, and the folk dance for the ballet-trained dancer by Massine.

Massine left Diaghilev in 1921 – an even greater loss than that of Fokine, who had revealed his full powers by the time he went, or that of Nijinsky, who had over-reached himself. It shows not only the strength of Diaghilev but also his truly creative gifts that he survived such losses and continued to shock the world. 'Shock meant progress – did not the first electric light and the first telephone shock?' And the collaborators who left him found themselves unable during his lifetime to create anything worthwhile. He had a monopoly. It was not merely that he fought tooth and nail to preserve it with all the skill of a great publicist and the ruthlessness of a tycoon. That alone would never have succeeded. His enemies would have rejoiced to see him fall, and Paris, unlike London, would not continue to applaud season after season just because after so many years he had become a grand old man. Their translation of the term would have been *ce vieux gâteux*. The fact is that every ballet bore Diaghilev's stamp. He selected the artists, teamed them, discarded them, took them back into the fold again. He suggested themes and criticised at every stage, and his was the final word. Possibly, after the early years, Stravinsky alone gave more than he received.

Diaghilev's only potential rival, Rolf de Maré's Swedish Ballet, founded in 1920, used many artists of the Paris school and also some of the Ballet Russe shock tactics. It lasted four years and left behind it some brilliant décors, particularly by Léger, but it created nothing of any lasting significance. It employed great artists but without the master touch.

Another failure, *Chout* (1921), may rightly be called 'magnificent'. Before the war, Diaghilev had heard of a musical prodigy, Serge Prokofiev, a pupil of Glière. In 1915 he commissioned a ballet from him, *Chout*, based on a Russian popular story. In the absence of a choreographer, Larionov, who painted the décors, did the choreography himself, assisted by a dancer, Thadée Slavinsky. The music launched the fame of Prokofiev; this remained one of Diaghilev's proudest achievements.

In the same year Diaghilev undertook his most costly experiment, a pious revival of the Petipa–Tchaikovsky classic, *The Sleeping Beauty*. The original production in 1890 had been a landmark in the history of the Imperial Ballet. It had rapidly become a popular favourite, though some of the critics were hesitant, calling the music 'serious and heavy, more for the concert hall'. Diaghilev was encouraged in his idea by Stravinsky, who felt with him that the time had now come to rehabilitate Tchaikovsky. He took an active hand in the production, entrusting the designing of the five sets with their elaborate machinery and over a hundred costumes to Léon Bakst. Stravinsky was asked to re-orchestrate the prelude and Aurora's variation from Act III, certain cuts were made and new numbers by Nijinska inserted. Diaghilev realised that only dancers trained in the great Russian tradition could do justice to a work that differed so greatly in style from his previous choreography. The keynote of the work was simplicity in the grand manner. He was able to recruit the greatest dancing talent of the day, with three Auroras

The Blue Train, 1924, the precursor of innumerable 'sporting' ballets with costumes by Chanel. The dancers seen here are Sokolova, Dolin, Nijinska and Woizikowsky.

Maquette by Marie Laurencin for *Les Biches*, 1924. This ballet by Nijinsky, so typical of the 1920s, has now been revived by the Royal Ballet with tremendous success as a period piece.

Maquettes for *Les Fâcheux* by Georges Braque, 1924.

'Night', curtain by Max Ernst for *Romeo and Juliet*, 1926. Many artists were scandalised at the participation of Ernst and Miró in an enterprise they considered 'bourgeois and commercial'.

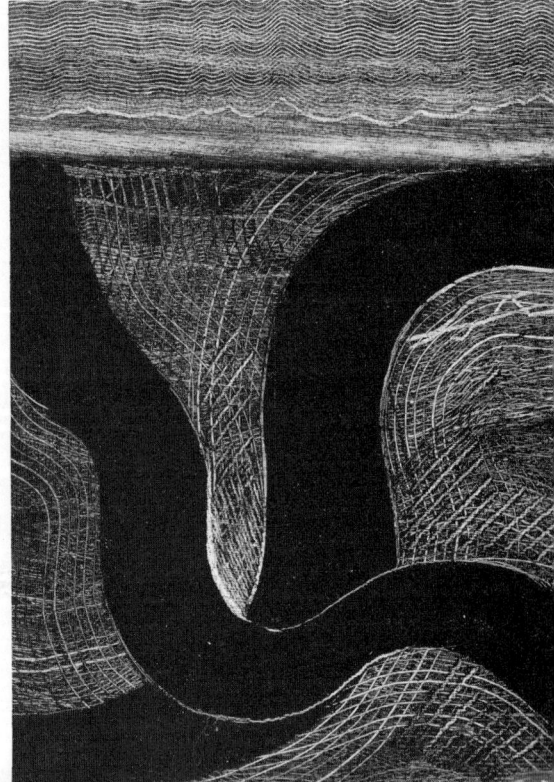

Hangings for the death scene in the same ballet. The music was by a young English composer, Constant Lambert. This marked the return of Karsavina to the Diaghilev ballet after the war and the revolution.

Successes and scandals

in the Maryinsky ballerinas Vera Trefilova, Olga Spessivtseva and Lubov Egorova, and with Pierre Vladimirov as Prince Charming. He induced Trefilova, one of the great generation of St Petersburg ballerinas, to come out from premature retirement. Spessivtseva, the last of the old régime and the first of the new, came to him from the Soviet Union. She was his ideal classical ballerina, his revenge on Pavlova. Lubov Egorova was later, with Preobrajenska and Kchessinska, to found the schools in Paris that brought Maryinsky school dancing to the west in the person of their pupils Toumanova, Baronova, Riabouchinska. It is also due to this revival that Russian dancing-schools were established in London and that their pupils were given a positive direction.

The première of *The Sleeping Beauty* was to be given in London, where the audience was more conservative than in Paris. To make sure of success Diaghilev had asked Stravinsky to write a reassuring introduction in the programme in the form of an open letter:

> 'It is a great satisfaction to me as a musician to see produced a work of so direct a character at a time when so many people who are neither simple, nor naïve, nor spontaneous, seek in their art simplicity, poverty and spontaneity . . .
>
> Tchaikovsky's music is quite as Russian as Pushkin's verse or Glinka's song.'

Unfortunately Diaghilev himself was less cogent and singularly tactless in a number of press interviews at the time in which he attacked Beethoven, greatly upsetting the music critics.

Possibly no classic has ever received a more lavish or better-danced production, but on the first night the machinery went wrong and there were many long pauses. And this was merely an aggravating factor; the real trouble was that the revival was a quarter of a century ahead of its time. Diaghilev had so accustomed his audience to shocks that they were unable to realise that all choreography was founded on this classic, that it was a basic part of Diaghilev's thinking and not a step backwards. The critics called it a Christmas pantomime and a French journalist wrote that it was more suited to the *Folies-Bergères* and far too poor to be played by an orchestra of repute. Only Diaghilev's greatest critical opponent, André Levinson, saw the point, calling it 'the boldest offensive of this intrepid man against stubborn prejudices that he himself had done the most to foster. Was it, as some misguided wag had said, "a restoration of the Romanov dynasty"? Was it a capitulation or a step towards freedom?' He went on to say that the acid test would be its Paris production.

Paris was never to see it. It ran for a few months, not long enough to recover its vast production costs, and left Diaghilev heavily in debt, with his whole enterprise in jeopardy.

Its subsequent influence cannot be exaggerated. More than any other ballet it pointed the direction that the art was to take in order to be firmly established when Diaghilev was no longer there to guide it. *The Sleeping Beauty* (characteristically Diaghilev had renamed it *The Sleeping Princess*, saying that he had no beauty available) was to become the corner-stone of England's national ballet when it was revived in 1939 with Margot Fonteyn in the title role. Night after night it was an inspiration to those who were to become the architects of The Royal Ballet. It set a standard of Maryinsky classical dancing to a generation who had not seen Karsavina and Nijinsky; it taught choreographers their grammar and syntax; it formed ballet critics as distinct from music critics; and it started the revival of Tchaikovsky.

Diaghilev never totally abandoned his fight for classicism, or for Tchaikovsky. A truncated version of *The Sleeping Beauty*, named *Aurora's Wedding*, proved immensely popular in London and Paris and remained so till the end. He mounted a one-act version of *Swan Lake* for Vera Trefilova in 1924 and in 1926, and in London, in 1929, for Alexandra Danilova and Olga Spessivtseva. This is not primarily a book about dancing, but these two great Maryinsky ballerinas, Trefilova and Spessivtseva, and the young Alexandra Danilova, who had only recently finished her training in the same school, played an important role in the history of ballet in the west. They arrived here at a time when dancing was rapidly becoming the weakest component of the ballet, and set a standard that remains valid to this day. They taught dancing to a generation of ballet critics, they proved that what was old in date was not necessarily old-fashioned, and that, on the contrary, classicism could renew itself with every generation. Spectators gradually came to recognise that it was only in these classics that they could judge the true worth of a dancer.

For once Diaghilev's judgment as a propagandist may have been wrong and he might have succeeded more rapidly had he started with these abridged versions.

9
The Last Years

The last years of Diaghilev's career, from *The Sleeping Beauty* to his death, were fruitful ones, though many people began to have their doubts about the direction he was taking, doubts brought about by the very classics which they had failed to accept. The work of this period is at present being reassessed through revivals that have generally proved timeless (and that are on the whole better danced than when they were first produced). It has obviously far from exhausted itself.

The year 1923 saw one of Diaghilev's greatest masterpieces, *Les Noces*, a collaboration between Stravinsky, Nijinska and Goncharova. It marked a return to his Russian roots, to a Russia of peasant life and village wedding-rites. It was acclaimed in Paris where Paul Dukas hailed it as 'the strangest and most powerful work we have seen since the Russians first started dancing here', but proved too austere for London. By way of contrast Nijinska provided two ultra-sophisticated works, *Les Biches* and *Le Train Bleu*.

The first of these was a masterpiece of skilled blending that wedded the talent of Poulenc and Marie Laurencin. It had no plot, but it indicated with great subtlety the attitude of the twenties to sex. Nothing was underlined, everything was there. It certainly belongs to its period, but it survives in the same way as a novel by Colette, and for much the same reasons.

The delicate *Les Biches* illustrates better than any other ballet the unity of Diaghilev's thought. It is quite inconceivable that it could be successfully performed without the original décors. Laurencin's pastel shades are a part of Poulenc's score. No Diaghilev ballet can be given in a different setting without

The Last Years

irreparable damage to the whole. Even when Benois himself designed a number of variants for *Petrouchka*, the work suffered considerably.

The other Nijinska ballet, *Le Train Bleu*, has dated beyond recovery, but it had a definite influence that still lingers on. It certainly made its mark on the music hall and operetta, besides opening up a new field, that of modern folk art. The idea was conceived by Jean Cocteau after seeing Anton Dolin performing acrobatics backstage; acrobatics but executed with all the style of a classical dancer. Cocteau saw the ballet as a series of picture postcards. The result was a sporting ballet with 'pop music' by Darius Milhaud. The style is described in an interview with Diaghilev:

Sketch by Goncharova for a group of female dancers in *Les Noces*

Design for *Les Noces* (Goncharova)

The Last Years

'You already know the poetry of machines, skyscrapers and other transatlantic manifestations. You must now accept this poetry of the street by taking in all seriousness the banality of its melodies. Don't be afraid of banality, give all your attention to the birth of this music, the music of tomorrow. Diaghilev's Ballets Russes, the artistic avant-garde of the world, cannot mark time, it cannot live yesterday's life nor even today's. It must anticipate tomorrow, guide the masses and discover what no one has discovered as yet.'

This not only explains Diaghilev's attitude, but reads like a manifesto before its time for 'pop art'.

In her choreography, Nijinska borrowed freely from the films in an amusing slow-motion sequence, copied numberless times since, and from the music hall. Film and music hall rapidly took back what she had borrowed and debased the currency. The ballet itself from time to time looks back at *Le Train Bleu*.

Nijinska's other ballet, *Les Fâcheux*, featured a magnificent décor by Braque and music by Georges Auric, but it never really came to life. It did, however, introduce a new collaborator, Boris Kochno, who became Diaghilev's right-hand man and who for a few years influenced him more strongly than anyone else. Kochno had immense talent; he nurtured the young Balanchine, and later Roland Petit, and wrote the libretto for most of the ballets of this final period. Apart from his gifts, he was young, and to Diaghilev, terrified of old age, this was a great attraction in itself. It was now, too, that his old collaborator Nouvel returned to the management.

It is possible that about this time Diaghilev began to doubt himself and to tire of the day-to-day business of the ballet. Now, too, Diaghilev began to reveal the full extent of his nostalgia for Russia, devoting more and more of his time to his collection of Pushkiniana and rare Russian editions. But he never lost sight of over-all strategy, and always remained in full control of artistic detail, criticising established artists as he did newcomers with a tone of authority they would not have accepted from anyone else.

Caricature of Cocteau and Bakst, by Bakst

Kochno's value to Diaghilev can be seen posthumously. He is the only person who for a short period successfully carried on the Diaghilev tradition. Cocteau apart, Kochno proved himself the greatest ballet poet of the age. He wrote the libretto for two Massine ballets, one of which, *Les Matelots* (1925), was the prototype for a fashion in popular entertainment. The music by Georges Auric was based on popular French songs. It had no narrative but dealt with the misadventures of three sailors on leave and was attractively decorated by a new Spanish painter, Pedro Pruna. It did for the seamier side of the port what *Le Train Bleu* had done for the fashionable *plage*. It was an immense success in a Paris accustomed to the *chanson réaliste*, but London found it too rough. Massine's other ballet, *Zéphire et Flore*, left little but a magnificent set by Braque and the launching of a young dancer, Serge Lifar, who was to rule the French ballet

The Last Years 105

scene for a quarter of a century and whose fidelity to Diaghilev's memory has been absolute. Nijinska's last ballet for Diaghilev, *Romeo and Juliet* (1926), was of more importance for what it led to than as a work of art in its own right, in spite of the fact that it heralded the return of Karsavina. It launched a very young English composer, Constant Lambert, and it brought to the theatre a collaboration between the painters Joan Miró and Max Ernst. The co-operation of these artists meant a great deal to Diaghilev. For a long time the Surrealist group had considered the Ballet Russe to be a bourgeois institution, which was as wounding to Diaghilev as it would have been to the most devout of communists. For this reason its première produced a scandal, the last one in Diaghilev's career and insignificant when compared with those of former years. The Surrealists considered themselves betrayed by their colleagues and there were cries of 'Judas', a rain of pamphlets from the gods signed by Aragon and Breton, and some scuffles. Thus up to the end Diaghilev played a role in artistic politics. The theme, a rehearsal of *Romeo and Juliet*, inaugurated a dreary series of backstage practice-costume ballets.

After the first period the Diaghilev ballet had been as international in its composition as the Ecole de Paris, but it had remained consistently Russian in one respect. The choreographers, though they had adapted themselves to the style of the painting and music of Paris, were all Russians, and (with the exception of Serge Lifar) had been trained at the Imperial Schools.

From 1926 onwards, with two exceptions, the choreography was entrusted to a man of outstanding skill and remarkable versatility, Georges Balanchine, who remains in the forefront of ballet to the present day and whose influence cannot be overrated.

Georges Balanchivadze, renamed Balanchine (he is Georgian by origin), was born in St Petersburg in 1904, entered the Maryinsky school in 1914 and joined the company on graduation. There he came under the influence of the choreographer

Goleizovski, and began his career at a time when the old traditions were already being questioned. He had had a thorough musical education and was an accomplished pianist. He went on tour in 1923 with a small group, among them Alexandra Danilova, and remained in Western Europe.

Choreography, then as now, was the branch of ballet for which it was most difficult to find suitable recruits. There could never be more than one choreographer at a time in a company, and the whole enterprise was at risk whenever a choreographer grew restive. Moreover, Diaghilev changed his direction so often that the choreographer was always being plunged into a new ambience which it was often hard for him to accept. Balanchine arrived on the scene at exactly the right time. Although he was only twenty-two years of age he had his own well-formed ideas, and Diaghilev played as little part in his formation as he had in the case of Fokine.

Balanchine produced eight ballets for Diaghilev, one of which was exceptional as being the only English contribution to the Russian ballet, and three of which have an assured position in history.

The English ballet, *The Triumph of Neptune* (1926), was based on the popular art of the cut-out lithographs for Pollock's toy theatre, and on the English pantomime tradition. The inspiration came from Sacheverell Sitwell and the score was written by Lord Berners: two old friends of the ballet. It was a complete success within its limited scope: it was truly national and fitted into Diaghilev's aesthetic of the moment, the naïve and popular treated with a touch of irony. Of far greater importance were *La Chatte* (1926), *Apollon-Musagète* (1928), and *Le Fils Prodigue* (1929). These belong to their period, but like Diaghilev's greatest works they are also timeless.

La Chatte, with a score by the twenty-five-year-old Henri Sauguet, brought a new kind of constructivist décor by Pevsner and Gabo, carried out in mica and American oil-cloth. This was to be copied in every type of production for the next decade,

Nijinsky making up for *Carnaval*, watched by Stravinsky (Cocteau)

invariably completely out of context. The story, or more properly, the theme dealt with the traditional balletic standby of metamorphosis, from cat to woman. But the treatment was entirely fresh, the setting providing an atmosphere of science-fiction – or rather, with the wonderful opportunity it gave to Diaghilev's speciality, stage lighting – science-poetry.

Another experiment in constructivism in the same year was entrusted to Massine. It was, so to speak, Diaghilev's challenge to the insulting appellation of 'bourgeois'. He set out to produce a Soviet ballet at a time when the Russians themselves were rapidly returning to classicism. In this sense it remains the only 'Soviet' ballet to have been shown in Western Europe.

The score for *Le Pas d'Acier* was written by Prokofiev, and the constructivist décors, in the Meyerhold-Tairov tradition, were designed by Jacoulov, one of the last *Mir Iskusstva* exhibitors. The ballet had no narrative; its two scenes contrasted the life of the peasant and the worker in the factory. The choreography was undistinguished, but the factory scene, later frequently imitated, was an exciting novelty, and the constructivist set greatly influenced theatre décors.

The two ballets that interested Diaghilev most during these final years were Balanchine's *Apollon-Musagète* (1928) and *Le Fils Prodigue* (1929). By now he was growing heartily tired of the seasonal struggle to be *dans le mouvement*. For nearly twenty years he had dictated fashion. Visiting the Paris exhibition of Arts Décoratifs in 1925, he spoke the simple truth when he said to the friend who accompanied him, 'This is a retrospective exhibition of the Diaghilev era.' Now events had speeded up, and an artistic novelty found its way into commerce within a few months. Moreover Diaghilev's health had broken down with the onset of diabetes. It is true that ballet cannot be in earnest the whole time; the satire and the *tableau de mœurs* had been thoroughly exploited. Diaghilev knew the value of his own works, though opposition often made him defend what he knew to be a failure. The time had come to call a halt to fashionable frivolities,

Danilova and Lifar in *Apollon-Musagète*, 1928.

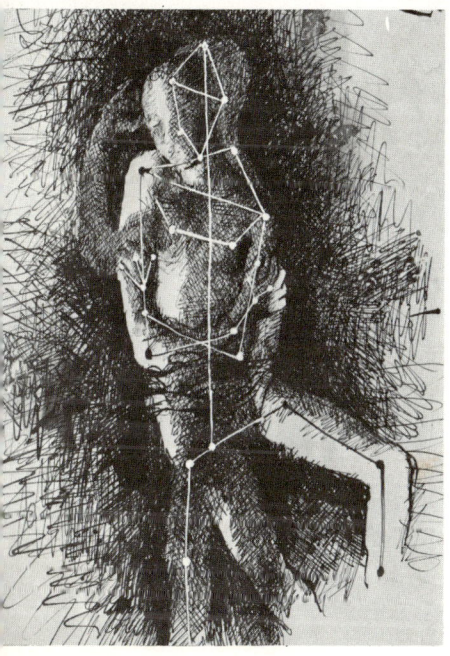

A drawing by Paul Tchelitchev for the Souvenir Programme of the ballet for the 1928 season. It was inspired by his costumes for *Ode*, his ballet of that year.

Olga Spessivtseva and Lifar in a one-act version of *Swan Lake*, given during Diaghilev's final season, in 1929, at the Royal Opera House, Covent Garden.

Décor for *Le Bal*, 1929, by Giorgio de Chirico.

Décor by Rouault for *Le Fils Prodigue*, 1929.

Diaghilev with Jean Cocteau, his friend and collaborator from the beginning.

The Last Years

however brilliantly they had been planned. '*Assez de musiquette.*' He was overjoyed when Stravinsky offered to write him a ballet on a subject of his own choice, *Apollon-Musagète*. It was especially welcome as Stravinsky was preparing a ballet for Ida Rubinstein's company, *Le Baiser de la Fée*, which Diaghilev looked on as an act of treason. His waning energies were restored, he left Kochno in charge of the lesser works and he was active with Stravinsky at every stage of the work. With great skill he selected a naïve *peintre de dimanche*, André Bauchant, to do the décors, in order to stress that this was something totally different from the pseudo-hellenism of the *Narcisse* of 1911. This was to be neo-classic where *Narcisse* had been neo-romantic. It was one of the outstanding successes of his career, and with it Balanchine launched a new school of choreography that went right back to the roots of classicism.

For the following year, the last, he had commissioned *Le Fils Prodigue* from his other great discovery, Prokofiev. Once again he was absorbed at every stage of its creation. For the last time he showed his mastery in matching music and décor when he selected in Georges Rouault the one painter in tune with the biblical subject and Prokofiev's dramatic score. This décor must rank with the greatest that the ballet has produced. In this return to a strong dramatic libretto Balanchine once more revealed his versatility. In these last two works Diaghilev had finished with snob appeal and was making a return to his basic principles. His next ballet was commissioned from Hindemith and there were plans for classical revivals.

In 1929 Diaghilev died in Venice after twenty years of absolute rule. His ballet died with him. 'Through the death of Serge Diaghilev,' wrote the Comtesse de Noailles, '. . . destiny has wiped out the brilliant frescoes that lit the grey universe.' Emile Henriot summed up his achievement when he wrote, 'The Ballets Russes renewed and gave a fresh youth to the theatre . . . the theatre that we had abandoned. Remember, remember the ugliness, the triteness, the parsimony, the mediocrity of the production and decoration at the beginning of the century.' Benois, at times, a grudging critic, underlined one aspect of Diaghilev's role: 'There was one thing missing in the generation of Russian artists who contributed to the creation of these superb manifestations of art, it was the will to create, that same will which Diaghilev possessed to such a degree. Diaghilev also had his special gift, *will-power*.' The critic-historian Julie Sazonova answers the vital question as to whether Diaghilev was truly creative or merely someone who assembled the ideas of others, by saying that his death proved conclusively what had been hidden during his lifetime:

> 'He had a creative genius; the elements that composed his ballets remain, but without him they no longer form a whole. We now know that Diaghilev's ballets were Diaghilev himself, that he intervened discreetly in all the artistic work and that he created the final result, a work that was personal and unique. We can therefore talk of his choreography.'

The truth of this summing-up has become more conclusive with the passing of time. Ballet did not die with him as many had prophesied, but it did suffer an amputation.

Sketch of Diaghilev by Cocteau

10
In Retrospect

Since his death in 1929, the society that Diaghilev knew and whose tastes he helped to form has largely vanished. The ballet that he founded and directed died with him, though a number of its creations still survive.

In most cases, when a fashionable and much-publicised artist dies his reputation sinks to a low level, sometimes, after a lapse of half a century, to be reinstated as a footnote to history. In Diaghilev's case one might have expected an almost total eclipse. There is no work signed by his name that can be taken from a library, played by an orchestra or attract a bid in an auction room. Yet the eclipse has never come. Instead, his fame has continued to grow – as one can see from the success of Mr Richard Buckle's admirable exhibitions in 1954 at the Edinburgh Festival and at Forbes House in London (where the run was twice prolonged), and also at the Sotheby sale of 1967 where costumes worn by his dancers attracted record prices. And in his native Russia, where for a long time Diaghilev was only known as an impresario and held in low esteem, he is at last beginning to be discovered.

The explanations for this are many. The first lies in the nature of the man himself. He attracted world attention in the pre-1914 Paris of Proust and the *salons*. His first audience was hand-picked; wealthy, aristocratic and highly sophisticated. He changed his direction and continued to change, in every case anticipating fashion and imposing his will. After 1918 his public was a new one; younger, poorer and more democratic. He taught this new generation to understand the movement in art that expressed its age. And it was a lesson in art-appreciation 'without tears'. The members of his audience might eventually have found their way into the art-galleries, but the glamour of the theatre was a first step. Picasso became a household word. Sometimes their appreciation was slow to develop. *Les Noces*, a comparative failure when first shown in 1923 (H. G. Wells defended it against a hostile press), was a triumph when revived by the Royal Ballet at Covent Garden in 1966.

It was the same with music. Stravinsky and Prokofiev, discovered and launched by Diaghilev, became familiar to thousands, who afterwards went to the concert-hall to hear their works. Also, it was largely through Diaghilev that Tchaikovsky earned a belated fame. Diaghilev was never over-sophisticated, like so many of his followers. He was not a *modernist* and he did not rely on stunts, though on many occasions his disciples and his critics took individual works, or some of their features, out of context for special effect. Diaghilev had a sense of proportion, and if he often cultivated the exotic blooms, he never neglected the roots.

At the present day ballet is more popular than at any time during its history. Except in the Soviet Union, contemporary ballet is a direct descendant of the movement that Diaghilev started. In England, Ninette de Valois and Marie Rambert, both brought up in the Diaghilev ambiance, laid the foundations of a national ballet. Constant Lambert, a Diaghilev discovery, played a major role as musical director and conductor. Frederick Ashton, the foremost English choreographer, came under the influence of Massine and Nijinska in the Ida Rubinstein company, an offshoot of the Diaghilev Ballet. In France, Serge Lifar revivified the Opéra, attracting many of Diaghilev's colleagues. The most inspiring revolt from the Opéra, the Roland Petit *Ballets des Champs-Elysées*, was guided by Boris Kochno, Diaghilev's right-hand man for so many years. Roland Petit has continued in the same spirit. The first Ballet Russe of Colonel de Basil and René Blum, founded in Monte Carlo in 1931, was headed by Kochno, Balanchine, Massine and Serge Gregoriev, Diaghilev's stage-director from the beginning. Its first creations made use of many

Drawing by Larionov of himself, Prokofiev and Diaghilev at a rehearsal at the Théâtre Gaité Lyrique in 1921

of Diaghilev's artists, and its repertoire was filled with Diaghilev revivals from all periods. In the USA, Balanchine restored the ballet to an importance which it had not had since the romantic period.

There is, however, one great difference between Diaghilev's ballet and ballet today which underlines his outstanding role. At present people go to see dancing rather than the entity that ballet should be. The painter's role in England and the United

States has sunk to a very low level. In Russia it is almost non-existent. The choreographer and the *maître de ballet* are in sole charge.

Diaghilev was never a revolutionary where dancing was concerned, and at the time of many of his most exciting experiments, when he could no longer draw from the Maryinsky and the Bolshoi, the level dropped sharply. It was Anna Pavlova who upheld the banner of classical dancing and who inspired the potential dancer. Today dancing has reached a very high level both technically and artistically, and it is the dancer who keeps ballet alive in a largely classical repertoire.

The great public tends to resist anything that is new, however good it may be. This is because there has been no consistent policy that can be felt to come from the personality of one man as it has developed over the years. Ballet follows fashion and does not dictate it.

Ballet today exists as something on its own, quite separate from the theatre, the art-gallery and the concert hall. It has no influence on anything but itself. The choreographer is his own critic. To paraphrase Clemenceau's well-known dictum, 'ballet is far too important an activity to be entrusted to dancers'.

It is possible that a Diaghilev could not have survived at the present day, and that the harsh realities of economics would have overwhelmed him. The large travelling company is no longer possible. The most recent one, run by the millionaire Marquis de Cuevas, did nothing more than provide lavish entertainment. Though the name of Diaghilev was so often invoked, the Marquis was looking at the distant past with nostalgic self-indulgence. Even when he commissioned décors from Dali nothing new was evolved; an oversized Dali painting merely dwarfed the action. It was cashing in on Dali's fame or notoriety. Diaghilev would have first discovered and then tamed him.

His influence lives but there can be no second Diaghilev.

Notes on further reading

BENOIS, A. *Reminiscences of the Russian Ballet*, London, 1947.
BUCKLE, R. *In Search of Diaghilev*, London, 1955.
CHUYOY, A. *Fokine's Memoirs*, London, 1961.
GRIGORIEV, S. L. *The Diaghilev Ballet 1909–1929*, London, 1953.
HASKELL, A. L. *Serge Diaghilev*, London, 1934.
KARSAVINA, T. *Theatre Street*, London, 1930 and 1948.
LIEVAN, A. *The Birth of the Ballets Russes*, London, 1936.
LIFAR, S. *Serge de Diaghilev*, London, 1940.

Index

Académie des Beaux Arts, 35
Académie des Sciences, 49
Academy of Art, 28, 30
Acis and Galatea, 58
Aksakov, 28
'Ambulants, The', 29–30, 33, 55
Animated Tapestry, The, 58
Apollinaire, Guillaume, 90
Apollon-Musagète, 106, 108, 113
Arensky, A. S., 59
Art Treasures of Russia, The, 36
Ashton, Frederick, 116
Assemblées Religieuses et Philosophiques, 36
Astruc, Gabriel, 11–14, 56, 59, 62, 80
Auric, Georges, 90, 103–4
Aurora's Wedding, 98

Baiser de la Fée, Le, 113
Bakst, Léon, 27–8, 34, 54–5, 59, 63–4, 69, 70, 75, 77, 83, 89, 92
  sketches by, 31, 104
  sketches of, 63, 104
Bakunin, M., 57
Balakirev, M. A., 75
Balanchine, Georges, 103, 105–6, 108, 113, 116
Balanchivadze, Georges, *see* Balanchine
Ballets des Champs-Elysées, 116
Baronova, 97
Basil, Colonel de, 116
Bauchant, André, 113
Bebel, A., 57
Benac, André, 15

Benois, Alexandre, 12, 27–8, 31, 34, 36, 38, 40, 53, 58–9, 70, 74–5, 83, 101, 114
Berners, Lord, 72, 106
Biches, Les, 100–2
Birlé, Charles, 27
Blanche, Jacques Emile, 72
Bloomsbury movement, 72
Blum, René, 116
Bois Sacré, Le, 74
Bolm, Adolf, 61
Bolshoi Theatre, 118
Boris Godounov, 12, 30–1, 59
Borodin, A. P., 59
Boutique Fantasque, La, 89
Brahma, 50
Braque, G., 103–4
Briand, Aristide, 12
Brillant, Maurice, 61
Brussel, Robert, 77
Buckle, Richard, 115

Caillavet, Arman de, 74
Callot, Jacques, 84
Calmette, Gaston, 77
Camondo, Isaac de, 15
Carnaval, 64, 107
Casse Noisette, 37
Cecchetti, Enrico, 14, 78–9, 84
Chaliapin, Feodor, 12, 31
Chatte, La, 106, 108
'Chinchilla', 11
Chopiniana, 58–9
Chout, 89, 92
Clemenceau, G., 118

Index

Cléopatre, 59, 70
Cocteau, Jean, 13, 61, 75, 80, 90, 101, 104
  sketches by, 63, 70, 73, 78, 81, 107, 114
  sketches of, 13, 31, 104
Contes Russes, 89
Coppélia, 35
Coq d'Or, Le, 82
Courbet, Gustave, 29
Covent Garden, 116
Cuevas, Marquis de, 118

Dalcroze, Jacques, 80
Dali, Salvador, 118
Danilova, Alexandra, 98, 106
Daphnis and Chloë, 75-6
Debussy, C. A., 35, 77-8, 80, 82
Degas, 29
Delacroix, E., 29
Delibes, L., 38
Derain, A., 89
Deutsh de la Meurthe, Henry, 15
Diaghilev, Sergei Pavlovich,
  ambitions of, 30, 33, 75, 99
  ancestry of, 24
  appearance of, 11
  appreciation of, 115-18
  art collection of, 31, 103
  art historian, as, 49-52, 54-5
  birth of, 24
  boyhood of, 24-6
  businessman, as, 32
  character of, 9, 11, 25, 27-8, 32, 34, 36, 38, 62
  classicism and, 79, 98
  composer, as, 30
  death of, 12, 113-14
  editor, as, 37-8
  enthusiasm of, 13-14, 69
  friendships of, 12-13, 30, 62
  ill-health of, 108
  parents of, 24
  pianist, as, 25
  role of, in ballet, 56, 71-2, 78, 82, 84, 91-2, 97, 103, 105, 108, 113-14
  showman, as, 35, 50, 60-1
  sketches of, 14, 31, 70, 78, 83, 114, 117
  university, at, 27-9
  war, during, 84
  women and, 62
Dieu Bleu, Le, 75
Dolin, Anton, 73, 101
Dukas, Paul, 100
Duncan, Isadora, 39, 40

Eclogue, 77
Edinburgh Festival, 115
Edwardes, Misia, *see* Sert, Misia
Egorova, Lubov, 97
Egyptian Nights, 58-9
Elman, Mischa, 73
Empress, Dowager, 71
Ernst, Max, 105
Evans, Edwin, 72

Fâcheux, Les, 103
Falla, M. de, 91
Fauve movement, 83
Femmes de Bonne Humeur, Les, 89
Festin, Le, 60
Figaro, Le, 77
Fille Mal Gardée, La, 35
Filosofov, Dima, 25, 27-8, 33, 36, 53
Filosofova, Anna Pavlovna, 25
Fils Prodigue, Le, 106, 108, 113
Firebird, The, 60, 69
Fireworks, 69
Flers, Robert de la Motte-Ango, 74
Florence, 28
Fokine, Michael, 14, 57-60, 64, 69, 70, 74-6, 82, 91, 106
Fonteyn, Margot, 98
Forbes House (London), 115
Franck, César, 35

Index

Gabo, 106
Gauguin, P., 79
Gautier, Théophile, 61, 74
Genée, Adeline, 72
Giselle, 35, 70-1
Glazounov, A., 58-9
Glière, 92
Glinka, M. I., 59, 97
Goldoni, C., 89
Goleizovski, 106
Golovin, 12, 69
Goncharova, Natalia, 82, 84, 89, 100,
    sketches by, 101-2
Greffulhe, Comtesse de, 11, 54
Grigoriev, Serge, 58, 84, 116
Guermantes, Mme de, 11

Hahn, Reynaldo, 75
Henriot, Emile, 113
Hernani, 80
Herzen, A., 28
Hindemith, P., 113
Hogarth, 89
Hôtel de Paris, 72
Hugo, Victor, 80

Imperial Theatres, 37, 71, 75
Indy, Vincent d', 35
Invitation à la Valse, 74
Italy, 84, 89
Ivan the Terrible, 59, 60

Jacoulov, 108
Jeux, 82
Judith, 59

Kahn, Otto, 84
Kaline, G. F., 27
Karsavina, Tamara, 61, 70, 73-5, 98, 105
Kartseva, Panaieva, 24-5
Kchessinska, Mathilde, 37, 60, 73, 97
Khovantchina, 31

Kochno, Boris, 103-4, 113, 116
Korovin, Konstantine, 31, 34, 53
Kropotkin, 57
Kyasht, Lydia, 72

Lambert, Constant, 72, 105, 116
Landowska, Wanda, 12
Larionov, Michael, 9, 14, 83-4, 89, 92, 117
    sketch by, 83
Laurencin, Marie, 100
Légende de Joseph, La, 82
Léger, F., 92
Levinson, André, 49, 98
Levitan, 26
Levitsky, D., 49
Liadov, 60, 69, 89
Lifar, Serge, 70-1, 104, 116
Liturgie, 89
Lohengrin, 28
London, 72-3, 91, 97, 104, 117
Longhi, 89
Lopokova, Lydia, 69

Maid of Pskov, 59
Mallarmé, S., 77
Mamontov, Sava, 31
Maré, Rolf de, 92
Markova, 73
Maryinsky Theatre, 59, 64, 71, 97-8, 105, 118
Massine, Leonide, 55, 80, 82-4, 89, 90-1, 104, 108, 116
Mata Hari, 12
Matelots, Les, 104
Mayakovski, V., 90
Merejkovski, D., 36
Michailovitch, Grand Duke Nicolas, 53
Milhaud, Darius, 90, 101
Millet, J.-F., 29
Mir Iskusstva, see World of Art and *World of Art, The*
Miró, Joan, 105

Monte Carlo, 71-2, 116
Moscow, 30, 82
Moussorgsky, M., 12, 59

Narcisse, 113
Nelidov, M., 12, 54
'Neva Pickwickians', 27-8, 37
New Path, The, 36
Nijinska, 92, 100-1, 103, 105, 116
Nijinsky, Vaslav, 13-14, 61-2, 64, 69, 70, 74-5, 77, 79, 80, 82, 89, 91, 98
  sketches of, 70-1, 78, 107
Noailles, Comtesse de, 61, 113
Noces, Les, 89, 100, 116
Nouvel, Walter, 9, 27, 30, 34, 36, 38, 59, 103
Novgorod, 24
Nurok, 36

Opéra (Paris), 12, 63, 89, 116

Palais Tauride exhibition, 49-51, 53
Panaieva, Elena Valerianovna, 24
Parade, 89-90
Paris, 72, 75-6, 91, 97, 100, 104-5
Paris Exhibition (1906), 53-5, 83; (1926), 108
Pas d'Acier, Le, 108
Pavillon d'Armide, Le, 58-9
Pavlova, Anna, 13-14, 61, 69, 72-3, 97, 118
Pergolesi, G. B., 90
Perm, 24, 26
Petipa, M., 40, 55, 58, 69, 70, 92
Petit, Roland, 103, 116
Petrouchka, 74, 90, 101
Pevsner, 106
Pharaoh's Daughter, 40
Picasso, P., 55, 79, 90, 116
Poiret, Paul, 64
Polignac, Princesse de, 12
Pollock's toy theatre, 106
Polovtsian Dances, The, 60

Pope, The, 84
Poulenc, F., 90, 100
Pourtalès, Dowager Countess of, 80
Prélude à l'après-midi d'un faune, 77-8
Preobrajenska, 97
Prince Igor, 59, 60
Prokofiev, Serge, 89, 92, 108, 113, 116
Proust, Marcel, 11
Pruna, Pedro, 104
Pulcinella, 90
Pushkin, A., 30, 32, 80, 97
Puvis de Chavannes, 29, 31

Rachmaninov, S. V., 35
Raffalovitch, André, 15
Rambert, Marie, 80, 116
Ravel, M., 35, 75-6
Réau, Louis, 55
Redon, Odilon, 78
Repine, 29
Respighi, O., 89
Riabouchinska, 97
Rimsky-Korsakov, N. A., 30, 59, 63, 82, 89
Ripon, Marchioness of, 72
Rodin, A., 78
Roerich, Nicolas, 79
Romeo and Juliet, 105
Rosenberg, L. S., *see* Bakst, Léon
Rossini, G., 89
Rothschild, Henri de, 15
Rouault, Georges, 113
Royal Ballet, The, 98, 116
Royal Opera House (London), 72
Rubinstein, Arthur, 12
Rubinstein, Ida, 59, 64, 113, 116
Russlan and Ludmila, 59, 60

Sacre du Printemps, Le, 80-2, 90
Sadko, 31
St Petersburg, 30, 74, 82
Satie, E., 55, 90

Index

Sauguet, Henri, 90, 106
Savina, 73
Sazonova, Julie, 81, 114
Scarlatti, 89
Schéhérazade, 63–4, 70, 75
Scherzo Fantastique, 69
Schumann, R., 64
Scriabin, A.N., 35
Serov, V., 31, 34, 59, 61
Sert, Misia, 12–13, 60, 62
Sitwell, Sacheverell, 72, 106
Skalon, W. V., 27
Slavinsky, Thadée, 92
Sleeping Beauty, The, 37, 60, 92, 97–8
Sleeping Princess, The, 98
Snegourochka, 89
Smolny Institute, 49
Sokolova, 72
Soleil de Nuit, Le, 89
Sources de la Musique Contemporaine, 36
Soviet ballet, 108
Spain, King of, 84
Spectre de la Rose, Le, 73–4
Spessivtseva, Olga, 70–1, 97–8
Sportsman's Sketches, A, 28
Stanislavsky, 31
Strauss, Richard, 35, 82
Stravinsky, Igor, 69, 74–5, 77, 79, 80–1, 84, 89, 90, 92, 97, 100, 113, 116
  sketch of, 107
Surrealists, 105
Sylphides, Les, 59
Sylvia, 35, 38
Swan Lake, 73, 98

Taglioni, M., 59
Tannhäuser, 40
Tchaikovsky, P. I., 25, 40, 55, 58, 60, 69, 92, 97–8, 116
Tchekov, A., 26
Tchcrepnin, 58–9
Tchernichevski, N. G., 29

Temps, Le, 77–8
Tenischeva, Princess, 34
Thamar, 75
Theatre Annual, The, 37–8
Théâtre des Champs Elysées, 80
Théâtre Sarah Bernhardt, 75
Tolstoy, Leo, 57
Tommasini, V., 89
Toumanova, 97
Train Bleu, Le, 100–1, 103–4
Trefilova, Vera, 97–8
Tretiakov, Pavel Mihailovich, 29
Tricorne, Le, 90
Triumph of Neptune, The, 106
Turgenev, I. S., 28

United States of America, 89, 117–18

Valois, Ninette de, 73, 116
Valse, La, 76
Vasnetsov, Victor, 34
Vaudoyer, Jean Louis, 74
Venice, 12, 28, 113
Verestchaguine, 29–30
Viardot, Pauline, 24
Vladimir, Grand Duke, 36, 54, 59–60
Vladimirov, Pierre, 97
Volkonsky, Prince Serge, 37–8, 40
Vsevolojsky, Ivan, 37
Vrubel, M. A., 31

Wagner, R., 28
Weber, C. M. von, 74
Wells, H. G., 116
Wilson, President, 84
World of Art, 27–8, 30, 35–6, 55–7, 74, 82, 108
World of Art, The, 33, 35–8, 49

Yuon, 12

Zaharoff, Basil, 15
Zassulich, Vera, 25
Zéphire et Flore, 104
Zucchi, Virginia, 40

GV
1785
.D5
H28
LEE